WORKING THE HALLS

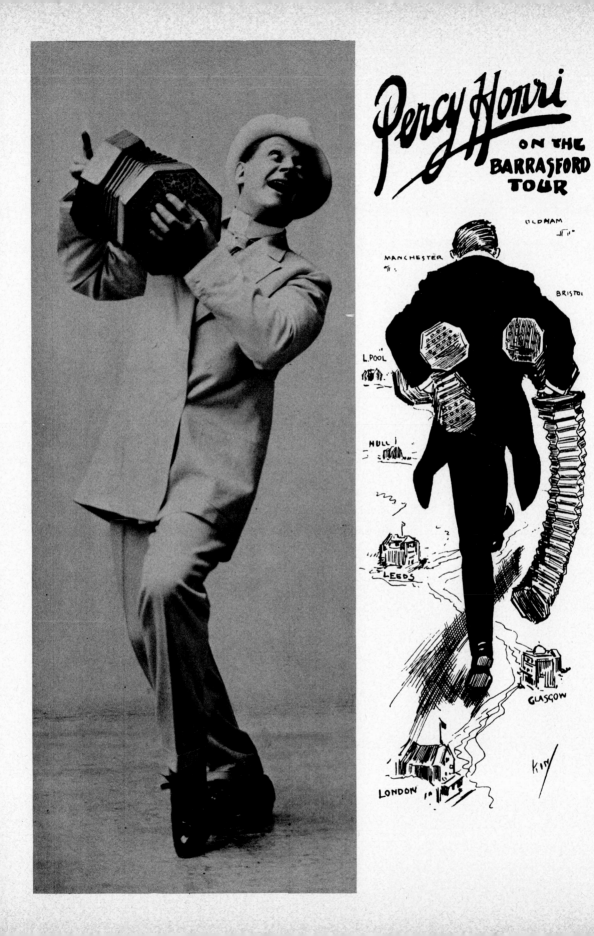

peter honri presents

WORKING the HALLS

THE HONRIS
in
ONE HUNDRED YEARS
of
BRITISH MUSIC HALL

OVERTURE
by SPIKE MILLIGAN

DÉCOR
by HELEN GRANT FERGUSON

PRODUCED

by SAXON  HOUSE

SAXON HOUSE
D. C. Heath Ltd.
Farnborough
Hampshire
England

ISBN 0 347 00013 4
Library of Congress Catalogue Card Number 73—10626

Photoset and printed in Malta, by St Paul's Press Ltd

To my own June Bernice
— and the fifth generation
Sarah * Caroline * Paul
With my love

PROGRAMME

BLACK AND WHITE ILLUSTRATIONS

BLACK AND WHITE ILLUSTRATIONS

WORKING THE HALLS

ILLUSTRATIONS IN COLOUR

Colour section between pages 88 and 89

I OVERTURE

THIS book has come along at a time when the first dust is settling on an incredible and exciting era in the history of popular entertainment. I mean the Music Halls. The post-war generations, filled with pop and TV, are growing up with no conception of the period that began with gas-lit stages and ended in the tense days before World War II. A few etchings and paintings by Sickert are the only colourful evidence we have of a great age.

There are still people who recall those days, but their number is dwindling. My own father, who appeared at Collins' and the Garrison Theatre, Woolwich, and my grandfather, who was a scene-shifter at Collins', both passed on tales to me; and I, in turn, did fin de cycle appearances at the 'Met', Edgware Road, and the Palace, Chelsea, so I suppose I am among the last in the line going back to those halcyon days.

The old theatres, alas, are now being pulled down at a tremendous rate. Even the 'Met', which after the destruction of the Holborn Empire was London's most central music hall, has gone — and this, surely, should have been saved as a souvenir of an age that will never come again. But those who sit in high places are often so remote from reality that disasters like this can occur and no one bothers to complain.

Happily, into the empty space now steps young (so to speak!) Peter Honri, who comes from a family that did much to keep music halls alive with their interest, vitality and love. His book bears witness to this; and it is crammed with so much information that, apart from being an engaging story, it could almost be used as an encyclopaedia of Music Hall history. He evokes all those haunting occasions — and one can feel the excitement — when the crowds converged on a damp night in winter to see their favourite stars, the working classes rubbing shoulders with the toffs and mashers, the news vendor shouting out the horrors of the Crimean or South African war, perhaps to be echoed inside by the top of the bill singing 'The Boers have taken my Daddy'.

The book is a treasure house of information and photographs (many of them unpublished till now). It mentions not only the stars but also those small supporting acts that toured around year after year, never getting any higher on the bill but vital to the profession. The book, as you can guess, has an emotional range, from sadness to hilarity, which in itself is representative of the period.

Peter Honri has really done his homework and research in putting this book together. It's the kind of book you can read right through or open at random, highly entertaining and readable — not only for doting theatre-lovers but by any standard — and on top of that, very educational. I personally loved the little cameos with which it's studded . . . but I won't tell you any more, just go ahead and enjoy it all, as I did. Or, if you don't, pick a convenient cliff and jump off it; you never know, you might get a laugh — you need one. Over to you.

Spike Milligan

THE HONRIS

Harry Thompson *1850–1937*
(Harry Tomps)
COMEDIAN
top right

married

Mary Horwood *1852–1914*
(Mary Thompson, Marie Mandeville)
'SERIO'
top left

their son

Percy Honri *1874–1953*
(Percy Thompson)
CONCERTINIST-ENTERTAINER
centre left

married

'Nan' Broadhead
MUSIC HALL PROPRIETOR'S DAUGHTER

their daughter is

Mary Honri
ACCORDIONIST-SOPRANO
centre right

and their son

Baynham Honri
FILM & TELEVISION CONSULTANT

married

Dorothy Wilkins
ACTRESS

their daughter is

Pinkie Honri
SOUBRETTE

and their son

Peter Honri
CONCERTINIST – ENTERTAINER
bottom left

married

June Bernice
ICE SKATER
bottom right

Percy and Peter Honri 1933 & 1951;
The Bar at Collins' 1957; Peter Honri as the mad ringmaster,
Collins', 1948 with Jimmy Patton and Joyce Clark

2   AD LIB TILL READY

WITH a flurry of cymbals and a final roll of the tymps, the overture ends. The musical director turns to face the spotlights that until now have played on his back, and smilingly acknowledges the clapping audience. He has broken through the slight air of stiffness that every audience has as it settles down to an evening's entertainment. He nods to some of the regulars; after all, he and most of the band are local men.

In the foyer, the house manager shepherds in the stragglers with a smile. Whilst he has complete confidence that the 'bill' will go well, he is aware that in music hall every Monday is a first night. Backstage, the resident stage manager checks the time the overture finished and flicks the switches that will send the heavy plum house tabs swirling up, creating a haze of dust that is caught by the spotlights as they pan up and across to where the opening act on this week's bill waits keyed up for that initial impact on Monday night – first house. Lighting dimmers slide to 'full up' as the band strikes up the first few bars. The satin front runners shimmer in the reflected footlights as they open. Simultaneously the proscenium indicator board's panel of bulbs changes from '1' to '2'. Mechanically the stage manager enters the exact time on his report sheet. The show has begun all over again – there will be laughs and excitement, memories and colour, songs and dances, for these are the people who work the halls.

Back in 1864, at the age of fourteen, one of my great-grandfathers made his music hall debut near Banbury; in 1886 another great-grandfather built his first music hall at Blackpool. The Thompson family, later the Honri family, are performers, whilst the Broadhead family were builders and music hall proprietors. The two families were linked when my grandfather Percy Honri married Annie Broadhead on 3 December 1902. This is my music hall pedigree – an unbroken line of performers for over a century.

On 2 February 1948, I started at the Middlesborough Theatre Royal as a fledgling pro in a touring revue, *Youth and Laughter*. The entire cast were teenagers, and the young principal comedian was Jimmy Patton. He is now one of the popular

Patton Bros act, and we have worked together a number of times. In a letter to me that week, Grandpa Percy Honri recalled his debut with his father in 1879 and wrote:

> ... An audience quickly appreciates a good tryer and you will remember seeing the act that your Auntie Mary and I put over with such unbounded success, so much so that we were able to stop the show at every performance. ... From my earliest appearance as a little boy of five years of age ... I have always been a 'show stopper', simply because on going on the stage I put my feet firmly on the floor boards and make up my mind with the resolution 'Now you've got to have it'. And that 'got to have it' slogan together with the memory of that little boy who is sitting on the back row of the Gallery and he wants to hear every word – every word, I am saying – did the trick!
>
> On two occasions when I was running my big show (*Concordia*) which formed only a portion of the programme there happened to be on the same bill a juvenile act of about twelve boys in an interlude called *Casey's Court*. In amongst this party was a very earnest lad who went through his paces as tho his life was dependent on it. True he was only getting five shillings per week pocket money and his keep but when I tell you the lad's name was Charlie Chaplin you will perhaps appreciate the fact that you have got possibly a better chance than he had to show your abilities.
>
> This letter, dear boy, seems a sermon in a way, but I want to impress upon you that there is possibly no one on this earth that wishes you greater success than we of Cut Mill so try, try, try and keep on trying. Managements are willing to pay a Thousand Pounds per week for personalities and personalities are only at the feet of the performers who – try.
>
> Keep the name of Honri flying to gain all the respect that your Father and Grandpa have managed to obtain, so far.
>
> Always your anxious
>
> Grandpa.

But *Youth and Laughter* was no *Casey's Court*, though I did get ten times Charlie Chaplin's money, worked the 'busy bee' gag and played a mad ringmaster in an ill-fitting red tail-suit!

For years the cry has gone up that music hall is dead – it is untrue. The tradition of music hall has gone far beyond the confines of the old 'Empires' and of the earlier music halls. Today one finds it in cabaret, pop concerts, theatre and films, and especially with television. It has never been the locale that has made variety truly the people's entertainment; rather it has been the performers reflecting their immediate era who have given life to this, the most ephemeral of the performing arts. The music hall artiste creates out of himself the persona that wins the laughs and the applause. Here is a virtually self-taught art that can never be perfected. Each audience is another peak to conquer, and the peaks are becoming harder as people grow more sophisticated. Always you remember you are only as good as your next performance; and that it's all been done before.

'You certainly look a classy audience tonight — why there's a fellow in the front row wearing a collar and tie. . . .

'Who are you? — Yes — you, waving the stick.'

'I'm the conductor.'

'How many on top then?' (Nice chap Frank. Wonder if he still wears carpet slippers in the pit? They look a nice crowd, even that Joe Miller gag went!)

Keep the ad lib going Frank — while the concertina gets the wind up . . . .

3

WE PLAY CONCERTINAS

'THAT's impossible – you can't come back as the same thing twice!' With that ripost, Chalk thumps Cheese on the back and the 'Somewhat Different Comedians' in their somewhat indifferent scarlet army tunics and off-white pith helmets take up their closing song:

> If you're wounded by a savage foe and bugles sound 'Retire',
> There's something in the British after all!
> You can bet your life, they'll carry you beyond the range of fire
> For there's something in the British after all!
> For although their guns be empty and their blood be ebbing fast,
> And to stand by wounded comrades means to fall...
> Yet they'll set their teeth like bulldogs and defend you to the last,
> Or they'll die like British soldiers after all!
> For there's something just a something rather difficult to name,
> Though her foes delight to call it 'British Gall'.
> But it's something that is something and it gets there just the same...
> There's something in the British after all!

Mr Rex Doyle bangs his gavel, and the two comedians exit. He is a popular chairman, and the audience is tightly packed in the small theatre to enjoy an evening of music hall. For each 'turn' Rex has an individual quip, and a burst of applause greets his sally at the expense of an Army private 'who is shortly to embark for South Africa and wishes to remain anonymous as he's with a lady'.

'Good luck, Mr Army Private, and don't forget that Lord Roberts wears galoshes to keep De Wet out! Every line a winner!'

Bang! His gavel punctuates the constant flow of music, patter and song; the turns are all old favourites, and the pert yet demure Angela Barlow who sings 'He isn't a marrying man you know...', the protean actor Andrew Jarvis and the rustic comedian Granville Saxton have all worked their acts, and taken their calls. The cheeky lyrics of 'Master' David Monico's song *Has anybody seen my tiddler?*, sung innocently in a Lord Fauntleroy costume and a large straw sailor hat, have merged into laughter and applause as he produces an enormous prop flounder that his rod could never have caught. As the applause dies away, distant bells are heard in the auditorium.

'The bellringers don't practise on a Friday night.' The chairman consults his watch, and mutters *sotto voce* into the wings 'Bats in the belfry, of course!'.

The bells grow louder, and it sounds as if every steeple in Farnham is rocking to their peals. The house manager, Mr Covell, hurries down the gangway. Mr Monico lingers. Miss Joan Coombes stops playing. The audience rustles and mumbles, as Rex Doyle listens to Antony Covell's excited message. With a whoop, the chairman springs to centre stage, and shouts:

'Mafeking has been relieved! Colonel Baden-Powell and his men are free! Cronje's beaten. It's true – Mafeking has been relieved. Three cheers for Colonel Baden-Powell and his men.'

Everyone joins in the cheers, and people pour on to the stage.

'So Cronje's beaten. Was it Mahon's column?'

'I don't know – all we know is that Mafeking's safe – Baden-Powell's safe.'

'We've got something to cheer about now. Mafeking is free!'

I start playing an instant parody of *Goodbye Dolly Gray* on my concertina:

> Goodbye Cronje we must leave you,
> Now that B-P's men are free.
> Two-One-Seven days it lasted,
> Now the Boers are forced to flee –
> Goodbye Cronje we must leave you,
> With that Creaky gun bust up.
> Mafeking, yes, Mafeking.
> Mafeking's relieved!

Everyone on the bill seems to be on stage now, joining in with my concertina. Outside there is cacophony of sound, cheering, the swish of rockets, an impromptu rendering by the town band of *Rule Britannia*. The whole house is singing in half a dozen different keys:

> Rule, Britannia! Britannia rules the waves!
> Britons never, never, never shall be slaves.

In fact, we are in the Castle Theatre, Farnham, May 1971; and that was an extract from the music hall show *Castle Music Hall, week ending May 19th 1900* that I wrote for Ian Mullins, the artistic director of the Farnham Repertory Company; however it was something like that in thousands of public places up and down the country on Mafeking Night – Friday 18 May 1900.

Charlie Coborn announced it from the stage of the Empire Theatre in Edinburgh, and during the matinee which followed Edward Moss asked him to read out Queen Victoria's reply to the Lord Provost's Loyal telegram of congratulation,

Week ending May 19th, 1900:
Peter Honri and Granville Saxton; the full company,
Courtesy the Farnham Repertory Company

Charles Coborn: 'Off she goes again!' © *Hutchinson Publishing Group Ltd*

Baden-Powell's home on Mafeking Day 1900

beɾore the newspapers published it. In a burst of patriotic euphoria – a trait seem-
ingly frowned on today by a public nurtured on thumbing its nose at the attitudes
of past generations – the old theatrical weekly *The Era* reported in its 'Music Hall'
gossip column:

> The week has been one of carnival, the current joy setting in on Friday the
> Eighteenth, with the glorious tidings of the relief of Mafeking. How the
> news was received has been told again and again in the dailies. In every
> Music Hall in London the announcement of Baden-Powell's triumph was
> given to the public from the stage; and amid scenes of indescribable enthu-
> siasm, *Rule Britannia* and *God save the Queen* were sung. Union Jacks seem
> to spring up everywhere as if by magic, round after round of cheers proclaimed
> the exultations so universally felt; and where portraits of the hero of the
> hour were exhibited the entertainment was kept at a standstill until delighted
> spectators had shouted themselves hoarse.
>
> At the Alhambra on Saturday, the night on which the relief of Mafeking
> was really celebrated, nearly 5000 people crammed the building. The one
> great attraction was not on the programme. Mrs Baden-Powell sat with her
> daughter and two sons in a box observed by all. At every pause there were
> demands that the mother of the hero should make a speech. When for five
> minutes the thousands yelled continuously their admiration at the picture
> of the great colonel, his mother sat quiet, contained, drinking in the praise
> of her son. It must have been a proud hour for her.
>
> To celebrate the welcome news of the relief of Mafeking, Mr Fred Holden
> had the Canterbury orchestra stationed in the vestibule the whole of Saturday
> afternoon, playing all the popular patriotic airs of the day. Vast and enthu-
> siastic crowds soon assembled, cheering and singing and rendering musical
> honours to the Queen, Baden-Powell and Lord Roberts.

On the Canterbury's evening bill Gus Elen continues to sing *The Boer of Befnal
Green*.

Tom Costello, hunting through the contents of one of his old travelling trunks,
finds the unused half of a return ticket to Pretoria from Johannesburg which he
forwards to 'Bobs' with the note 'You may find it useful'.

A new word 'to maffick' is put into the dictionary – a word that even now
echoes the escapism that the British will cling to, even though as they are doing
it they are aware that there's a 'morning-after' feeling to look forward to!

The Blue Post Hotel, in Martin Street, Stafford, is crowded when the news
reaches the town. The fair has been doing a roaring trade, especially the coconut-shy
where favourite targets are the Boer leaders' heads. Further down the street, the
Lyceum Theatre is patriotically decorated to match The Blue Post. The pub and
the theatre are run by two music hall artistes, Harry and Mary Thompson, my
great-grandparents. It's a double celebration for them, as their son Percy Harry
is spending a week with them before resuming his music hall tour as Percy Honri –

'The World's Greatest Concertinist'. This has only been his third visit in the two years his parents have lived in Stafford.

It was pantomime time – January 1972 – when a message came to my dressing room at Richmond Theatre recalling Stafford and The Blue Post. That was how I came to meet Harry Grattidge: 'I always go to see the Richmond pantomime for my birthday treat – the way you used that baby concertina, and coming out of that box like a jack-in-the-box – the jolly jester! The programme told me the rest. . . .'

This was Captain Harry Grattidge, O.B.E., lately commodore of the Cunard line, and captain of both the *Queen Mary* and the *Queen Elizabeth*, who wrote the book *Captain of the Queens* about his life at sea. He was born in Stafford, and was able to tell me a lot about Harry and Mary Thompson and the young Percy Honri.

Still hale and hearty in his eighties, he related:

'In those early days I used to be fascinated by the front-of-house manager, Mr Elphinstone, parading up and down and singing out in a very raucous voice "Early doors this way – thruppence". A few yards up Martin Street was Parker's, the pork shop, then Mrs Gee's pub The Fountain and then The Blue Post Hotel, the rendezvous of many of the Lyceum performers.'

I showed him some of the playbills of the Lyceum when the lessees were the Royal Thompson Trio. Prices ranged between 6d and 2s, and the bill of fare was three-day visits from touring players such as 'The Edwin Garth and Geo Bates Co.' in *McKenna's Flirtation*, with Mr Garth playing the milkman Michael Ryan, 'a part played by him over 700 nights'. When the 'Cowper-Calvert Company' came, their playbills announced: Thursday 22 September – *Ingomar* by Mrs Lovell with William Calvert in the title role; Friday 23 September – *Camille* by Alexandre Dumas with Clara Cowper in the title role. Their visit ended on the Saturday, when William Calvert would play 'Col Henri Farreau' in his own play, 'a grand military drama in four acts – *Life and Honour*'.

Captain Grattidge recalled helping the billposter and 'nearly falling into his paste bucket', and going in Great-grandpa's pony and trap to inspect the poster sites with Harry Thompson and his nephew Albert Lewis – who got billing himself as 'Billposter Inspector'.

'Mr Thompson tried to get mother to let me join the Trio as I had a rather lovely soprano voice at that time and sang solo at the church. But she positively refused. However the sound of Mr Elphinstone's voice made me think of the sea, and in 1906 I left Stafford as a humble cadet and joined a sailing ship, the *Osborne*, on a four-year voyage around the world. . . .'

By then the Thompsons had left Stafford and Percy Honri had launched his greatest musical sketch, *Concordia*. But on Mafeking Night, Percy had a 'week out', and what better for the twenty-six year old teetotal son of a music hall comic turned publican than to lead the customers of The Blue Post and The Fountain in a cheering, singing procession round the town's hostelries – to the music of his concertina.

Percy Honri

"SURPRISES EVERYONE."

Vacant
Dec 31
Jan 7
" 14
" 21
" 28
Feb 4

Under canvas: Percy Honri and friends 1898; *Era* advertisement, 1899; The Thompson Trio outside The Blue Post, Stafford 1900

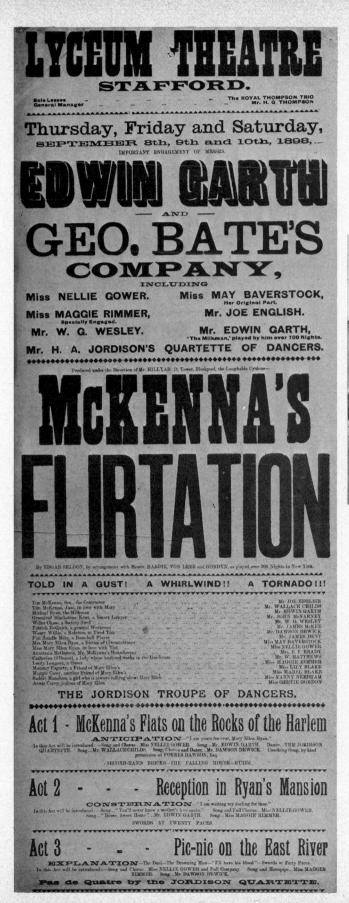

Lyceum playbill 1898; Harry Thompson inspects his poster display 1898

AND SHE SHALL HAVE MUSIC WHEREVER SHE GOES

There is a common misconception that music hall artistes were all Londoners or that maybe 'a few did come from Up North'; in fact the music hall performer came from anywhere and nowhere. From the gent to the gipsy, they could all be found within the profession. I suppose I could say that my great-grandparents connected with the music hall came from yeoman stock – the Thompsons of Banbury, the Horwoods of Thorpe Mandeville, the Broadheads of Mansfield and Blackpool, the Baynhams and Birches of Longsight.

Harry Thompson was born on 22 January 1850 in Banbury, the second son of William Henry Thompson, superintendent of Banbury police, and Jane Hutchings. His elder brother William opened the first cycle shop in Banbury, and was an important shareholder in the new Singer Cycle Company in Coventry. His younger brother Walter joined him as a performer at one time, but his talent was on the operatic side, and he emigrated to the United States, eventually becoming a leading tenor with the Mackay Comic Opera Co.

The connection with the Banbury area began in 1810, with the arrival of thirteen year old William Henry Thompson, from London Wall near Moorgate Street, who apprenticed himself to Mr Needle the chairmaker who lived at the Bull's Head Inn, later to be known as the White Hart. The population of Banbury was then 2,841. Today it is about 30,000. Banbury's first theatre was in a large barn behind a small brewery in the Horse Fair. It was regularly used as a theatre, particularly by the stock company run by Searle and King in the early 1820s, and after taking up the horn as a hobby, William Thompson formed, and played in, the orchestra of the theatre. One favourite piece was *The miller and his men* in which they used to introduce the effect of burning down a mill nightly. Often, too, he took his 'key bugle' on the Kidderminster–London coach and at one time he even thought of taking a guard's place permanently. But whilst the money was good at around £1 a day, the guard had to be up and the coach loaded to leave Kidderminster by 5 a.m. London was reached by 11 p.m., and the guard was able to go off duty around midnight. For the return journey, the coach had to leave by 5 a.m. again. So William decided to remain as a chairmaker, whilst augmenting his wage as a watchman. In 1825, he joined the day constables. He became superintendent in 1836, when municipal reform came into existence. By 1847 he was chief usher to the county court, and he held that post right up to his death in June 1891, at the age of ninety-four. During his lifetime he had witnessed the jubilee celebrations for two monarchs, George III in 1810 and Victoria in 1887. His membership of the Philharmonic Society at Banbury and his ability as a horn player had ensured a musical upbringing for his son Harry.

Harry served his apprenticeship as a butcher, and also tried his hand as an auctioneer; but eventually his prowess as a humorist at the local Oddfellows meetings made him forsake the red meat for the red nose. At twenty-two he was already fairly well known in the area as a comedy multi-instrumentalist. Harry enjoyed life to the full; an inveterate practical joker, he was a born wanderer and storyteller.

Riber　Karl　Grindoff　Claudine　*Riber dead*　Grindoff

Riber　Karl　*Miller*　Count Fribera　Friberg　Grindoff

'Penny plain': Plate 4 from
Webb's 'Characters in '*The
miller and his men*'; No. 11
from Webb's 'Scenes in *The
miller and his men*': the exploding
mill

About seven miles from Banbury, across the county boundary in Northampton-shire, is the still attractive village of Thorpe Mandeville. Back in 1252, the manor was held by Richard de Amundevil; in 1306 it was known as Throp Mundevill. In 1700, the name of Horwood appeared on the church register for the first time, and nearly two centuries later Mary, the twenty year old daughter of James and Ann Horwood, was courted by Harry Thompson. On 10 February 1872, Harry and Mary were married and went to live in a tiny semi-detached cottage which almost overlooked the church where so many Horwoods now lie buried. Harry was a restless young man; not for him the set, ordered life of his father or his father-in-law.

English village life in the 1870s followed a fairly prosaic pattern governed by the Fourth Commandment, but there was a wide variety of entertainment — travel-ling showmen with the fairs, barnstormers and itinerant musicians. Corn Exchanges and Oddfellows Halls echoed to 'blood and thunder' melodramas and banjo-twanging minstrel troupes. Here Harry had his grounding in the rough and tumble of the tavern and the smoking concert. The villagers of Thorpe Mandeville and its sister villages of Sulgrave and Greatworth worked hard and they played hard.

In January 1874 Disraeli became Prime Minister once again, and launched his 'sanitas sanitatum' crusade. The right of organised workers to take collective action was legalised, and the first Labour M.P.s, Alexander Macdonald and Thomas Burt, won Stafford and Morpeth. By tradition each village had its own great family — the Humfreys of Thorpe Mandeville, the Pargiters of Greatworth and the Wash-ingtons of Sulgrave. Lawrence Washington had been given his lands by Henry VIII in 1539, taking over the manor and lands of Sulgrave hitherto the property of the Monastery of Saint Andrew. Washington had settled in Northampton and even-tually became mayor of the town. He was the great-great-grandfather of George Washington.

NURSED ON BURNT CORK

The Thompson Trio might have been three brothers — but only Percy Harry sur-vived childhood. He was born at home in Thorpe Mandeville on 24 June 1874. His father was away at the time — he had gone off on one of his long journeys, either as a travelling auctioneer or in a 'fit up' show of some sort. He frequently did this, leaving Mary this time to take her newly-born son back to James and Ann Horwood. When Harry was home, he encouraged Percy to play with his unusual comedy musical props — the boy was bonny and enjoyed the garish colours of the materials that covered many of the mechanical contraptions his father had bought and made to add to his nigger minstrel act: 'The Original Black Cloud, Eccentric Jester and Funny Instrumentalist; At Liberty Concert Hall, Circus or Diorama.'

In 1951 I was to use 'burnt cork' myself on the sands at Hastings, while working as 'Mr Interlocutor' with Harry Orchid's Swanee Minstrels. During my summer season there, Grandpa and Grandma came over from Cut Mill to see me, and he confirmed that my make-up was: 'Up to standard — mind you, G. H.

Elliott always used champagne corks. Get a pile of corks, set 'em alight and then float the burnt corks in a basin. When the burnt cork has absorbed the water, and looks a little water-logged – squeeze 'em tightly (very messy this part, Peter) then fill up a jam jar with the mudlike paste. It dries quickly on the face with a fine matt finish.'

He knew the secret of making proper burnt cork, because he had been a minstrel himself, on 29 September 1879, at the age of five. The *Dudley Herald* of 4 October 1879 reported that the Oddfellows Hall at Great Bridge '. . . was crowded to excess by a fashionable and enthusiastic audience which comprised the elite of the neighbourhood'. The report went on to tell its readers that

> . . . anything likely to offend the eye or ear was studiously avoided, and an entertainment replete with good vocal and instrumental music and refined wit were the gratifying results which attended the desire to please and not offend the keen susceptibilities of a cultured audience. . . . Little Percy Thompson, aged 5 years, gave his noted clog dance and won rounds of applause for his extraordinary performances. . . . As corner men Messrs Thompson and Mallins were capital throughout the performance and their eccentricities provoked much mirth.
>
> Six months later, the Original Great Bridge Minstrel show provoked much laughter. . . . Messrs Harry Thompson (Bones) and J. Mallins (Tambo) kept the audience in roars of laughter by their quaint sayings and droll performances. Mr H. G. Thompson's banjo songs and dances were given in first-class negro comedian style, and his playing on the piano was much admired for its sweetness and execution. . . . Master Percy Thompson aged five years gave a song and dance in character with all the sang froid of a person of maturer years, his infantine performances being repeatedly encored.

In 1881, the Thompsons moved from Thorpe Mandeville into lodgings at 132 High Street, Cradley Heath – closer to the music halls of Birmingham. Harry's great friend Albert Virto lived here, and had told them that London agents like George Ware and Richard Warner were often seen at the local halls. Whilst it must have been a wrench to leave her beloved village, Mary packed up house and found that, involuntarily, she was now a wanderer. A deft needlewoman, if not very musical, she decided that if you can't beat them you can join them.

The journey to Cradley Heath was made by horse and cart – like Wild West pioneers, the Thompsons set out from Thorpe Mandeville with young Percy sitting on the tailboard and ensuring that nothing fell from the motley cargo: punch and judy frame and its full cast, harmonium, banjos, trombone, a mandolin, tubular bells, violins, flutes and penny whistles, assorted concertinas, two skips neatly marked 'Home' and 'Show' containing their personal belongings, a grandmother clock (the Horwoods' wedding present eight years earlier) and 'Patch', their dog. Percy practises some of Jack Ketch's patter from Harry's Punch and Judy routine – the 'schwazzle' is safely in his father's pocket, 'just in case the lad swallows it'. He already has a powerful voice:

Virto and Thompson 1881; Peter Honri in the Hastings
Swanee Minstrels 1951

ODD FELLOWS' HALL,
GREAT BRIDGE.

On Monday & Tuesday Evenings,
September 29th & 30th, 1879,
AN

ENTERTAINMENT

WILL BE GIVEN BY

The Amateur Minstrels,

CONSISTING OF

New Songs, Choruses, Dances, Stump Speeches, and Dialogues.

LITTLE PERCY THOMPSON,

(Aged 5 Years) will give his noted Clog Dance.

Artistes.

Mr. K. VAUGHAN. Mr. F. HICKIN. Mr. W. BOTT.
Mr. H. ELWICK. Mr. LISSEMORE. Mr. J. PHIPPS.
Mr. W. RODEN. Mr. J. ROBERTS. Mr. J. DAINTY.
Mr. H. WILKINS. Master P. THOMPSON.

Orchestra.

Mr. J. WOODHALL, 1st Violin. Mr. J. DAVIS, Cornet.
Mr. C. MILLS, 2nd Violin. Mr. J. PITT, Bassoon.
Mr. W. BEVON, Contra Bass. Mr. DOWNING, Flute.

The Entertainment will include the laughable Sketch,

"FIVE DOLLARS AND A NEW COAT,"

Concluding with "The Plantation Walk Round Emancipation Day."

INTERLOCUTOR	- - -	Mr. C. M. LEES.
BONES	- - -	Mr. H. THOMPSON.
TAMBOURINE	- - -	Mr. J. MALLINS
MUSICAL CONDUCTOR	- - -	Mr. J. WOODHALL.
MANAGING DIRECTOR	-	Mr. C. M. LEES.

Doors open at 7-30 p.m., to commence at 8 prompt.

Admission: Front Seats, 1/- (which may be reserved upon application to Mr. H. Elwick or Mr. C. M. Lees, Great Bridge) Back Seats, 6d.—Tickets to be obtained from any of the Amateur Minstrels—Mr. W. J. Morgan, Horseley Heath—Mr. J. Davies, Great Bridge—or any of the Odd Fellows' Hall Co.

CARRIAGES MAY BE ORDERED FOR 10-15 P.M.

Percy Honri in Naval costume 1882; 'day bill' of Percy's debut as a performer

'Now, Mr Punch. You are going to be executed by the British and Foreign Laws of this and other countries, and you are to be hung up by the neck until you are dead – dead – dead. Now, my boy, here is the corfin, here is the gibbet and here is the pall.' His voice changes to that of Mr Punch: 'There's the corfee shop, there's giblets and there's St Paul's.'

Whilst young Percy successfully worked turns between the classroom and the music hall, Harry had added to the strings of his bow by acting as a variety agent and composer, emulating George Ware who wrote *The Boy in the gallery*, initially for Nellie Power; later it was adopted by Marie Lloyd and became her earliest song success. As an agent Harry had some assorted clients, including 'Alexander and Payne – Champion medallists, jugglers, acrobatic skaters and negro comedians. See their great Glove Fight On Skates – the funniest act extant. Dec. 12th Star Music Hall, Barrow with Benefit. Monday next Tayleurs Circus, Swansea for Carnival on the Ice!'

The *Magnet* is quoted as saying 'their show throughout is unique, funny and original'; whilst 'Fanny Steel – the dashing and pleasing serio, characteristic vocalist and dancer with Good songs and Good Wardrobe' was now appearing with 'terrific success at Dexter's Varieties, Halesowen; re-engaged for March. Manchester and Bolton to follow.'

In the *Birmingham Mail* of 6 March 1882, the columnist states: 'Miss Vesta Tilley of the Birmingham Theatre Royal pantomime has accepted a song written and composed by Mr Harry G. Thompson entitled 'The Fisherman's Child' which she will produce with scenic and mechanical effects.' Whether Vesta Tilley ever produced the song 'with scenic and mechanical effects' I have no idea, but she certainly sang it, and Harry cashed in on the fact and persuaded Mr Harry Beresford of New Street, Birmingham, to publish it.

Now nine years old, Percy was a seasoned professional. His father and Albert Virto were working their double act 'Virto and Thompson, the Musical Savages' and had taken their comedy musical turn on a continental tour that included the 'Crystal Palace of Holland', the Paleis Voor Volksvlijt, Amsterdam, Musis Sacrum, Arnhem, Park Tivoli, Utrecht and the Folies Bergère, Paris. The idea of the nine year old Percy appearing at the Folies Bergère in 1883 has always been a favourite family joke with us. The tour was noteworthy because this was when the name 'Honri' first appeared. The spelling with an 'o' instead of the usual French 'e' in 'Henri' was due to a typographical error on the poster. Harry liked the shape of the new name 'Honri', and was aware of the impact of crisp billing on music hall posters. Five-letter names made for good layout – so 'Percy Honri' and later 'Harry Tomps' were born, and indeed Peter Honri. But my father Baynham had changed his name by deed poll just before I was born in 1929! A faded cutting, dated by Harry 24 March 1884, refers to the visit of 'Virto and Thompson' and Percy Honri to Paul's Concert Hall, Leicester. In his own autobiography *Fifty Years of Spoof*, Arthur Roberts tells of his first appearance at that same Paul's Varieties:

It was an old fashioned show and was almost as famous for its hot meat pies as it was for its variety artistes. I think this competition with hot meat pies made me a little nervous. Mr Paul's audience knew the qualities of the meat pies but they did not know me. The meat pies were things with an established reputation. So far as Leicester was concerned I had my reputation to make.

Dear old Mr Paul noticed my nervousness, so during the interval when the audience, according to habit and tradition, went downstairs to purchase meat pies, he made the following speech from the stage:

'Ladies and gentlemen,' he said, 'I must ask you tonight to be on your best behaviour. I want you all to be good – good, damn good. Now you know I always get a very fine show for you. I always do my best to entertain you with the best turns. The very best, ladies and gentlemen, that the British Empire can supply. Now tonight, I have got Arthur Roberts coming on in a few minutes. I have got him from London and I can tell you that Arthur Roberts is the best comic singer in the world and that is the reason why I want you to give him a chance. He is the best comic singer in the world, I tell you, but – but – I have got a better one coming next week!'

After that extraordinary speech of introduction it was a very difficult ordeal to face that Leicester audience. . . .

On the Thompsons' visit to Paul's Varieties, top of the bill was Hyram Travers, the coster comedian who had a complete mastery of cockney backslang and pre-dated Gus Elen, Alec Hurley and Albert Chevalier. The report states that 'Mr Percy Honri' brings descriptive and topical songs, and there is '. . . a series of drolleries, highly grotesque and ludicrous provided by Messrs Virto and Thompson, who manage to evoke musical strains from instruments not usually employed in selected orchestras, and go through a number of feats which are particularly catching'. No doubt the prefix 'Mr' replaced the usual 'Master', because Percy was singing his father's song *If I Were a Man*.

Immaculately clad in evening dress, the 'Pocket Sims Reeves' as his letterheads read, steps into the sputtering limelight. He is nearly ten, and soon his billing will be the extravagent 'Champion Boy Tenor of the World'. His clear voice cuts through any noise, and music hall audiences were usually noisy. The boys at his school this week will ask their fathers if they saw Percy Thompson at Paul's Varie-ties. Albert and Harry, the burnt cork still apparent behind the ears and under their chins, watch him from the wings with Mary Thompson, proud of her 'early turner'. Percy smiles back at them and then, taking the downbeat from Mr Potter, starts to sing the song his father composed for him:

> I am sure I'm pleased to see you all here,
>> It gives me the greatest delight;
> With your best attention to amuse one and all
>> A few topics I'll sing you tonight.
> I am ten years of age in June '84,

"THE FISHERMAN'S CHILD."

Written and Composed by *Harry Thompson*.   Published by *Beresford,*
Birmingham.

Dear mother, let me hear your voice,
I feel so sad to day,
And the time it seems so very long
Since father went away.
I wish he would return to us,
The day seems long and drear;
The winds are whistling loud and shrill,
There's something wrong, I fear.

CHORUS.

I cannot close mine eyes to sleep,
No footsteps can I hear;
I wish our father would return,
Our gloomy home to cheer.

He said he'd not be long away
When he left us at the gate,
His boat was ready near the rock,
His nets and lines were straight.
He kissed us all, and said, "Good bye,
I shall return to tea;"
And Willie laughed to hear him say—
"I love the foaming sea."

The hours passed on, no father came,
We could hear the breakers roar,
So we sat and thought his little craft
Was wrecked and washed on shore.
Next morn, upon the beach, we stood,
And strained our eyes to see,
When lo! his body came in sight—
A lifeless corpse was he.

Song sheet and original manuscript for Harry Thompson's song,
The fisherman's child; Harry Thompson; Vesta Tilley

PERCY HONRI,
THE WONDERFUL INFANTINE TENOR
POCKET SIMS REEVES, TOPICAL & CHARACTER VOCALIST, ORIGINAL SONGS,
Beautiful Appearance, Splendid Voice,
HAS APPEARED AT THE
PRINCIPAL LONDON AND PROVINCIAL HALLS.

Above, Percy Honri's first letterhead
Left, Percy as 'The Fisherman's Child'
Right, Arthur Roberts

Far left, Percy as 'the Pocket Sims Reeves'
Left, Percy wearing some of his 'benefit performance' medallions

But I'll do the best that I can,
To relate my ideas in the simplest way,
    What I'd do if I were a man.

The first thing I'd do, if I had the power,
    I'd help a poor man that was down,
And give to him all the assistance I could,
    And never upon him would frown.
There is many a man, who, in life would do well,
    If you'd encourage him all that you can,
Take him by the hand, and give him a start,
    That's what I'd do if I were a man.

How many poor children you meet in the street,
    Quite friendless, half clothed, and half fed,
With no one to help them or speak a kind word,
    Or earn them a mouthful of bread.
Now if any rich man wants to make a big name,
    To come to the front is his plan,
Let him build a good home, and these street Arabs feed.
    That's what I'd do if I were a rich man.

The war that's been raging with Egypt of late
    I hope will soon come to an end;
Commanders were thoughtful, our troops were all firm,
    Our rights they will ever defend.
General Gordon deserves a hearty good cheer
    For his courage out in the Soudan,
For his true British pluck, I wish him good luck,
    He's a noble true-hearted good man.

Our Members of Parliament deserve a good cheer,
    On which ever side they may be;
They are men who all in the land should be proud,
    Though their ideas do not always agree.
I am sure it's the secret of all our success
    To have Gladstone to draw out the plan.
You can't find one better if this world you search through,
    I hope I shall grow such a man.

During the interval, when members of the audience bought their hot pies, for One Penny' they could buy this 'descriptive and topical' song in a two-page 'Percy Honri Song Book' with four other sentimental or patriotic songs. Next year, Salisbury would replace Gladstone in the eulogy, whilst Gordon's death would be mourned. I don't suppose the atmosphere has really changed, as I found out in 1960 when I worked one of the Leicester social clubs with my concertinas.

During my act the chairman rang the bell to announce 'Hot pies is ready!'
ENTER THE THOMPSON TRIO
Today the accent in light entertainment of all kinds is on presentation, on the spectacular. Gone for ever are those loners who week after week honed and polished their acts from Plymouth to Aberdeen, men with rose-pink complexions, Cherry Blossomed bald pates, plus fours and corncrake voices; the women, ever younger then Somerset House would have them be, kittenish or stately and ever ready to parry an 'I' for an 'I'. Gone for ever, that's the P.R. man's line, but a thousand club nights prove him wrong. In a later chapter I outline some of the changes wrought in music hall entertainment. The popularity of the pastiche 'old time music hall' is only partially linked to that B.B.C. success story *The Good Old Days*. And what a debt performers owe to Barney Colehan, and to Don Ross! After the last war, Don's *Thanks for the memory* gave the older performers a base for their talents and new generations a chance to see real music hall. Television has engendered a more intimate style, and a modified technique is essential. With music hall it has brought the audience back as part of the show.

Harry Thompson and the other Victorian performers in every type of entertainment constantly thought about the presentation of their turns, of being 'the unique act', of being 'the original'. Back in the 1880s, music hall was still basically a pothouse entertainment, but even if their surroundings were tawdry and backstage comforts non-existent, most turns wished to be known as 'refined'. The week commencing 7 July 1884, the 'Champion Boy Tenor of the World' was appearing at the tiny New Gaiety Palace of Varieties, Tithebarn Street in Preston. I have a copy of the poster, and for variations in type and number of words it would seem that Mr Harry Hemfrey, 'Sole Proprietor and Manager', liked his money's worth from the Herald Printing Works in Fishergate! There are 454 words, including the name of the printers and, as for Mr Paul's show at Leicester, the whole British Empire has been scoured to supply Preston's entertainment.

NEW GAIETY PALACE OF VARIETIES
Tithebarn Street, Preston
Sole Proprietor & Manager: Mr Harry Hemfrey.
Stage Manager & Scenic Artist: Mr Joe Stoner.

———

An entire new company this week
Fresh faces and old favourites this week!
And every evening. MONDAY JULY 7th 1884 During the week
Doors open at 7·15; Overture at 7·45; Saturdays half-an-hour earlier
Most expensive engagement and first appearance
in Preston for six nights only of
The Wondrous
PANLOS

❊ Programme. ❊

☞ Each Number will be shown from the right-hand side of Stage, corresponding with that in this Programme indicating the name and particulars of business.

1. Overture—Band.
2. John and Maggie Coleman.
3. James Merritt.
4. Little Tich.
5. Arthur Alexander.
6. Peggy Pryde.
7. Katie Lawrence.
8. Harry La Rose.
9. Sam Redfern.
10. Sergeant Simms and Troupe of Nine Boys.
11. James Fawn.
12. Brothers Griffiths and their Blondin Donkey.
13. Chirgwin, the Kaffir.
14. Mons Trewey.
15. Nelly L'Estrange.
16. Chas. Sutton.
17. Katsnoshin Awata, the Imperial Japanese Court Juggler.
18. Marie Loftus.
19. G. W. Hunter.
20. The Schaeffer Troupe of Acrobats.
21. Sam Torr.
22. Cee-Mee, Unrivalled Aerial Gymnast.
23. Lily Grey.
24. Sweeney and Ryland.
25. Millie Zara.
26. Ella Zuila, the Australian Funambulist, and Little Lulu.
27. Frazer an Allen.
28. Nelly Power.
29. The Three Champions—Dan Leno, Hugh Dempsey, and J. Coleman.
30. Brothers Horne in Sketch, Sullivan's Arrival.
31. "Vento."
32. Prof. Wingfield and Performing Troupe of Dogs.
33. Katie Seymour.
34. Thompson Trio.
35. Pierce and Monaghan.
36. Raffin's Pigs and Monkey.
37. Frank Maura, Equilibrist.
38. Brothers Borani.
39. Sisters Phillips and Brothers Lorenge.
40. Henderson and Stanley Quartette.

41. The Musical Gartos.
42. Alex Staunton.
43. Rosse Heath.
44. John E. Drew.
45. Maud Distin.
46. Dutch Daly.
47. Sisters Du Cane.
48. Jennie Leslie.
49. The SUCCESSFUL SKETCH, entitled 'THE DEVIL BIRD,' introducing Millie Hones, Fred Williams, Leo Stormont, and Mrs. George Fredericks.
50. Leglere Troupe of Acrobats.
51. Harriett Vernon.
52. Arthur Roberts.
53. God Save the Queen.

❖ ARTISTES ❖

Appearing at the London Pavilion, Royal Aquarium, South London Palace, and Gatti's, appear by special permission of their respective proprietors—

MESSRS. E. VILLIERS, DE PINNA, POOLE & ULPH, And MADAME GATTI.

❖ THIS ❖ PROGRAMME ❖

Has been arranged by the kind co-operation of the following gentlemen—

Messrs. H. J. DIDCOTT, R. WARNER, E. COLLEY, PERCY WILLIAMS, GEO. WARE, VICTOR & TURNBULL, and F. HIGHAM of HIGHAM & LEWIS.

General Manager and Stage Director—MR. A. THIODON.
Musical DIRECTOR—MR. E. BOSANQUET.
Secretary—MR. A. TRESSIDDER.
Machinist—MR. PIKE. Property Master—MR. A. JACKSON.
Gas Engineer—MR. BLISS. Lime Light by T. WELLS.

Music Hall pros' outing to Clacton 1888: Mary, Percy and Harry are to be found in the third row back; Programme of Canterbury Music Hall's 4th Anniversary under Crowder and Payne's management 1887

The Thompson Trio: above, in London; below left, 'Refined Musical Jokers'; below right, introducing Percy Honri, 'Champion Boy Tenor of the World'

Sensational acrobats, including
Little Ernest! The Midget Clown
Don't miss these artistes.

———————

First appearance and for 6 nights only of Miss
KATE LEE
Serio Comic Vocalist

———————

Engagement for 6 Nights only, of Master
PERCY HONRI
The Champion Boy Tenor of the World!
All should hear him! A Novelty!!

———————

Engagement for 6 nights only, of your old favourites HARRY
RUSSELL
and YOUNG
DEUTCHER
The famous Dutch Entertainers and Tyrolean Minstrels!
In their favourite impersonations
Harry Russell's melodies are the prettiest of the day.
Harry Russell's songs are hummed and whistled everwhere.
Hear Young Deutcher in his American song and dance.
Hear Young Deutcher as a Tyrolean singer.
See Young Deutcher as Little Schneider.
See Young Deutcher in his self-taught hornpipe.
A big Novelty and a hearty laugh for all.
Harry Russell and Young Deutcher surpass all other Dutch
entertainers.

———————

First appearance of Mr
HARRY MARTIN
The Musical Momus in conjunction with
MR LEVITE
In their new and original entertainment.

———————

Most important engagement and for 6 nights only of
LEVITE'S COMBINATION
PANTOMINE TROUPE

Some of the London Music Halls advertised in *The Entr'acte*, December 1893; Alfred Bryan cartoon of Jenny Hill, 'the Vital Spark'

in their Sensational Ballet entitled
'MISCHIEF'
With new scenery and effects.

———————————

FRIDAY. Monster attractions for the Benefit of Mr J. Graham
(Graham & McBride) who was suddenly stricken down with paralysis
on May 2nd, and since then has been unable to follow his profession.
THURSDAY. Laidies FREE night if accompanied by a Gentleman.

———————————

Reserved Seats: 1/- Sides & Promenade 6d; Pit 3d.
Doors open 7-15; Overture at 7-45 Half price to Reserved Seats
at 9 o'clock (also promenade, Saturdays & Benefits excepted)
SPECIAL NOTICE – Pass Out Checks are not transferable.
Seats not guaranteed. No money returned. Police in attendance
and strict order enforced. Children must be paid for.

———————————

The Herald Printing Works, Fishergate, Preston.

There is no trace of the New Gaiety today, but it is my belief that this entire 'bill' was Harry Thompson's company. His skating acrobats Alexander and Payne he re-named The Panlos, engaging Little Ernest in Preston for the week; Fanny Steele became Kate Lee; Harry himself worked whiteface as the song-writing Harry Russell, with young Percy Honri doubling up as 'Young Deutcher', and finally he worked 'blacked up' as Harry Martin 'the Musical Momus' with Albert Virto as 'Mr Levite'. The Levite's Combination Pantomime Troupe was a marionette show which he had exchanged for his punch and judy frame. That sad announcement of the Friday Benefit for the stricken Mr Graham, and the warning that police would be in attendance and 'strict order enforced', underline the social conditions and behaviour of those days.

Sometime between Preston in July 1884 and the Rochdale Circus of Varieties on 10 October that year, Albert Virto left the Thompsons and Mary was persuaded to join the act – her name is to be Marie Mandeville, and her lack of musicianship may be a handicap as the act is a musical one. Percy is now playing sufficiently well on the trombone and concertina to take over much of Virto's business. So Mary learns to play the bells, not by notes or even numbers, but on a highly original word notation 'door-window-door-door-door'. The bells are concealed in large fans.

Harry and Percy hid musical instruments in prop chairs; a property dog's stomach became the bellows of a concertina; a miniature concertina nestled in an enormous bow tie that Harry wore. There was a clockwork train that ran on stage, and could be played as a trumpet. A drawing room setting was toured to fit the piano that Harry always featured, and this was the foundation of the Thompson

Percy Honri, 'the Crown Prince of the concertina'; medal presented to Percy by Professor MacCann 1891

Trio act for twelve years. Mary was foil to the low comedy of Harry with the check comedy pants and ginger wig. Percy, in velveteen suit and lace collar, would initially appear aloof from his father, but the climax of the act would find them all playing a rousing march — a complete antithesis to the refined setting. At Rochdale, they got a good press for their first week:

> The Thompson Trio produce a sketch in which Mr Thompson works with unflagging zeal; he plays very creditably on a variety of instruments, a solo on the piano being especially well rendered; and a youthful member of the trio, Percy Honri, sings 'The Death of Nelson' in such a manner as to make him quite a favourite. George Beauchamp's eccentric make-up provoked hearty laughter, which was not lessened by the low comedy in which he indulged.

The Thompson Trio soon established themselves as the 'refined act that managements wanted to book', and the dates flowed in. They gave 'value for money' and 'they always bring something new'. Richard Warner was now their agent, and Harry, Mary and Percy worked hard to make sure 'their performance was not one to be missed'. The years passed and the voice of the 'Champion Boy Tenor of the World' was starting to break. His grandfather had given him a programme of Signor Guilio Regondi's visit to Banbury. Regondi was a virtuoso of the concertina in the 1850s and 1860s, and had composed two concertos for the 'English' concertina. It was the volume of sound possible from that small box that intrigued the young Percy. In a press interview he gave forty years later, he said:

> A shilling — that's all it cost me — at any rate to get the first step on the slippery slope that leads either to Top o' the Bill or Edge o' Beyond.
>
> You see my father happened to possess common sense. My voice was bound to break, so he suggested I should learn some instrument — the piano or the violin. What did I fancy?
>
> I fancied the concertina, overcame my father's dismay, bought a shilling piano catechism — and here I am, Percy Honri 'the concertina man'.

WORKING TURNS

For the actor, London is the goal. The performer regards it as another date to be 'pencilled in' or 'confirmed'. For him the attraction of London used to be that you could 'work turns' — that is, appear at a number of music halls each evening and thus increase your salary. In the 1880s most halls ran 'once nightly', with programmes of upwards of twenty turns, and it was not difficult to arrange contracts at several halls the same week, often changing en route in the hansom.

The 'Full Tops' and 'Full Bottoms' would hire their broughams at £3 per week when working turns at four halls a night. Bessie Bellwood sang a song about *The Pro's Coachman* at the Pavilion in the '90s:

> First he's on at the Tivoli
> Then he's on at the 'Pav'.
> Then comes out and begins to shout:
> 'Fifteen minutes you have!'
> Back again to the Paragon,
> Then again to the Royal...

Warner arranged bookings for the Trio at a number of London halls, and with lodgings fixed at 115 Stamford Street, SE, the Thompsons were working turns in various permutations between the following music halls: Deacon's, Albert Palace, Cambridge, the Middlesex, Foresters, Harwood's and the South London – 'Just to keep us alive' quips their regular card in *The Era*.

Deacon's Music Hall had been enlarged some three years earlier and now had a capacity of over a thousand. Sam Sutton was chairman, and he and the new owner, Captain Davis, were two of the most popular men in Finsbury. The Albert Palace was a large concert room at the west end of the Albert Exhibition Building in Prince of Wales Road, Battersea Park, whilst the Cambridge in Commercial Street, Shoreditch, owned by William Ridley, could hold up to two thousand. The Middlesex, known as the 'Old Mo' after the Mogul tavern on which it was built, now belonged to J. L. Graydon and could hold twelve hundred patrons. The house in Raglan Street, with a three-hundred-seater music hall on its first floor, was known as Foresters. The South London Palace was in Lambeth, and Harwood's in Hoxton.

Cockneys have always had a soft spot for the concertina, so Harry made sure that it was well featured in their turn – the Thompson Trio now could truly term themselves a 'concert-in-a turn'.

The *Era* critic obviously intended to be exact and lyrical in his review of Deacon's *Week ending July 2nd 1887*: 'The good attendance habitual to Deacon's since it has been under the rule of Captain Davis seems to keep up in spite of the high register of the thermometer and the strong counter attractions out of doors when "Leafy June" bathes the landscape in sunshine.' The pros reading *Era* on the Sunday journey must have smiled at this description of 'leafy' Finsbury. Our lyrical critic admires Jenny Hill 'who is more juvenile, more vivacious, and funnier than ever...' and goes on:

> Miss Hill's immense fund of animal spirits exerted its well known spell upon the audience, who could do nothing but laugh heartily while she sang 'The wedding of Robinson's son'.... For Miss Hill it is an artistic triumph, one that emphasises her many-sided histrionic talent. Mr Walter Munroe, who is in full training for the mile and half mile races at the music hall sports, demonstrates his right to the title of Irish comedian by tuneful songs... but he should, we think, assert himself more as a character actor... but Mr Arthur Forrest should immediately avoid the trick of shutting his eyes when singing.

It is absurd, and spoils his otherwise comic efforts. The Sisters De Laine . . . accentuate their success by a skipping rope dance, which takes immediately. The Thompson Trio, in the course of a slight sketch, introduce much fun and more music and singing, Master Percy Honri specially distinguishing himself by his rendering of a patriotic song. The concertina trio constituted also a most acceptable final item in their entertainment and it is rare indeed on the music hall stage to hear that much-abused instrument so well played, and the performers so readily acknowledging the necessities of both time and tune.

A faded pink programme reads:

Celebration of the Queen's Jubilee, Friday 15th July 1887. Andrew Mitchell Torrance Esq., Chairman. Programme of Entertainments at the Freemens Orphan School, Brixton to commence at half past six o'clock. Lieut. Frank Travers will give his Extraordinary Ventriloquial Entertainment entitled 'The Colonels Evening Party'. The Thompson Trio in their Refined and Funny Instrumental Music, Wit, Comedy, Fun; and in their Laughable Speciality Act 'The Black Music Tutor'. Poluskie and Blackell 'The Grotesque Acrobats' in their Burlesque Military gymnastic instruction. Carl Hertz the King of Clubs and World renowned conjurer The Vanishing Dickey Bird. Professor Bridges' famous Punch & Judy with their dog 'Toby'. The celebrated Domestic Drama. At the piano: Mrs W. R. Pope. The entire entertainment provided by, and under the personal direction of Mr William Holland, Albert Palace.

But Banbury calls. William Thompson is now 90 and the Thompson Trio is due to take a well-earned rest after 419 consecutive performances without a break. They fulfil their outstanding 'dates' and in September 1887 return to Bridge Street, Banbury. Percy Honri has now developed as a virtuoso concertinist: '. . . Percy Honri's fine solo "The Lost Chord" on his duet concertina brings down the house. . . .' Already Sir Arthur Sullivan's tune becomes a part of Percy's life. At Grandpa's funeral, many, many performances later, I was proud to play that moving melody which then became part of mine. We look upon the concertina as our family instrument, and there are many types of concertina. They may look alike — that 'old threepenny bit' hexagonal is common to them all. But the 'English', the 'Anglo' and the 'Duet' each have a different keyboard. Harry played two concertinas of the 'English' system — a treble and a tenor-treble whose ranges were similar to the violin and viola. His 'bow-tie' concertina worked like a mouth-organ, and was known as a miniature Anglo. Percy was attracted by the full organ-like chords possible on the duet system invented by J. H. MacCann of Plymouth, in 1884. This was a newly patented variation of Charles Wheatstone's original duet system. It was a difficult instrument to master, but Percy was not deterred, and soon the baroque cadences of his MacCann duet concertina dominated the family act.

MacCann had appeared in music halls and at concerts since the 1860s, usually billed as 'Professor' MacCann, 'King of the Concertina'. In April 1891, the great MacCann presented Percy Honri with an engraved silver medal 'for his marvellous playing on the duet concertina'. The ceremony took place at Hengler's Cirque, Liverpool, where the Thompson Trio had a fortnight's engagement. Thus did the reigning concertina king acknowledge his successor.

Percy Honri, the young Soloist

4   WE BUILD MUSIC HALLS

'MR EX-MAYOR and gentlemen of the Council ... Words fail me when I try to thank you for the many kindnesses I have received at your hands during the nine years I have been a member of the Blackpool Town Council, and more particularly do I feel a difficulty in finding words to acknowledge properly the very great honour you have conferred on me this day...'

The sea winds howl around the Council Chamber, and the icy December rain beats a constant tattoo on the window-panes. With great dignity, the bearded Alderman W. H. Broadhead, J. P., takes office as Mayor of Blackpool for the coming year of 1906.

He was my great-grandfather, the owner, at that time, of ten music halls which he had built himself and which he ran with his two sons, William Birch Broadhead, known as 'Willie', and Percy Baynham Broadhead, familiarly known as 'P.B.B.'. His circuit never paid the huge salaries that the 'big tops' could command, and that were paid by Edward Moss and Oswald Stoll, so the pros used to call the Broadhead circuit the 'Bread and Butter' tour.

'... No one can love the town more than I do, or can have gained better health from residing here, or can have greater faith in its continuous growth in the face of any and all opposition.' The new mayor is no native of Blackpool. Born the son of a Mansfield farmer in 1848, when he was six the family moved to Nottingham where young Broadhead remained at school until he was fifteen. He decided he wanted to be a builder, and so he began learning the business of a builder – a business that took him all over the country, but in particular to Longsight near Manchester where he met and married Mary Anne Birch in 1871. The building firm of W. H. Broadhead was first established near Stevenson Square and Tib Street in Manchester that same year. He came to Blackpool with his young family for health reasons, and in 1886 acquired the Prince of Wales Baths on the Promenade, deciding to include entertainment as well as recreation in the bill of fare. That inaugural mayoral speech of Great-grandpa includes the customary eulogies of Blackpool's achievements to date, but his shrewdness in publicity matters is apparent when he continues drily:

W. H. Broadhead's first 'hall': Blackpool's Prince of Wales Baths; Mary Broadhead and William Broadhead, Mayor and Mayoress of Blackpool 1911

Top, left, Willie Broadhead; top, 'Nan'; top far right, interior of the Baths, middle centre, 'P.B.B.'; centre far right, the Broadhead sisters and Mrs Willie Broadhead; bottom right, Willie, his family and parents

> ... the company-house keepers can aid the Advertising Committee very
> materially, and themselves at the same time, by having on their notepaper
> and business circulars printed views of our grand and spacious promenade.
> Illustrations of pictures do more to attract by showing the town as it really
> is than any other method. I am sure this means of drawing additional visitors
> would amply repay those making a trial. . . .

The new mayor had four daughters besides his sons Willie and P.B.B. They
were Annie, Kate, Alice and Hilda. Whilst they were a close-knit family, only
Nan and Kitty were involved to any great extent with their father's and brothers'
theatrical activities. Willie was the driving force in the growth of the circuit. On
leaving Blackpool Grammar School, he helped his father develop the Baths as an
entertainment centre. A champion diver himself, Willie frequently appeared in
the aquashows and competitions held there. In 1896, he supervised the building
of the Royal Osborne Theatre in Oldham Road, Manchester. This was so successful
that the firm expanded and built the Metropole and Junction Theatres, and the
Hippodromes at Hulme, Queen's Park and Salford and the King's at Longsight
near his mother's home. The Broadheads built music halls at Preston and at Bury
as well. But on 3 March 1907, Willie died from pneumonia. He was only thirty-
four. The music hall journal *Encore* said:

> He was journeying during the night in a covered car, but an accompanying
> car broke down, and in stopping to render assistance, Mr Broadhead got
> wet through. Our correspondent informs us that he was much worried over
> the Music Hall strike, and it was while returning from London on business
> in connection therewith that he caught the chill which terminated fatally.
> Mr Broadhead was a hard worker and personally conducted the most
> important business of the theatres. He was often to be seen motoring from one
> 'Broadhead' house to another. . . .

Over three hundred mourners attended the funeral, and the massed bands of all
the family theatres headed the cortège playing Chopin's 'Funeral March'. Willie
was an intensely practical man, and was proud that all the theatres included the
latest electrical switchboards, and that their facilities were the equal of the leading
halls of the country. P.B.B., the surviving son, took over his late brother's mantle.
Percy Broadhead had a lawyer's mind, and in 1913 he headed the group of independent theatre proprietors who formed themselves into the Provincial Entertainment Proprietors and Managers Association. This body was later to be known as
the Independent Theatres Association, and P.B.B. was its president from 1913
until his retirement in 1948. He was a doughty fighter for the independents
against the pressure of the big circuits.

The Broadhead music hall acumen developed from their personal involvement
with the fortunes of their first music hall — the Prince of Wales Baths. The
Thompson Trio first appeared there in 1886, when their musical 'knockabout'
act had complemented the antics of the watershow clowns; and it became a frequent

Above, programme detail, Royal Thompson Trio at the Prince of Wales Baths; above right, song cover; right, letterhead

'return date'. An 1890 penny song sheet tells us there were three performances daily, at 11, 2.30 and 7.00, and that

> The Management desire to draw attention to the fact that they have at great expense constructed a new CENTRAL STAGE, extending the width of the Bath, on which Variety Performances are given at each Entertainment in addition to the Swimming Show and Water Pantomime. No expense has been spared in securing the best Artistes now before the public. . . . No Intervals. No Tedious Waits. An uninterrupted 3 hours Show. The Sight of Blackpool.

The first Broadhead house exemplified an aspect of music hall at that time, its close relationship with circus and with watershows. The showmen of that era welded these triple native talents to provide spectacle. Drums were banged — pictorial posters pasted up everywhere, and then the spangled aerialists spun a hundred feet above the gaping audience.

It was on that central stage that the Thompson Trio worked with the added title of 'Royal', after appearing before H.R.H. the Duke of Cambridge at the Cavalry Theatre at Aldershot on 17 April 1890. The *Hants and Surrey Times* reported that the Duke

> . . . entered the theatre by a carpeted and covered way, the band of the 19th Hussars struck up a few bars of the National Anthem, and the cheering became deafening. His Royal Highness gracefully bowed his acknowledgements, took his seat in a lounge chair, and appeared greatly interested in the performance, frequently expressing his approval by the words 'Very good, very good indeed'. . .

In *The Era* of the following week, Harry Thompson revised the Trio's regular 'card' advertisements, and tacked the Duke's verbatim comment on to the review of the show where Percy Honri's 'manipulation of six different instruments at one time was greatly admired by His Royal Highness and the remainder of the distinguished company'.

The *Military Gazette* dwelt at length on the deep interest His Royal Highness

> . . . takes in the amusement and recreation of the soldier, as well as in his comfort, welfare and efficiency . . . the fact that the Commander-in-Chief lent his patronage to the entertainment provided in this large and well conducted establishment speaks more than words for the affection he entertains for the men who have the burden on their shoulders of upholding the country's honour in its most trying hour, viz, when the sword has to be drawn. . . .

The phrase 'gone to be a soldier' no longer meant 'gone to the bad', and the popularity of Rudyard Kipling's stories and poems undoubtedly helped to remove the stigma of unpopularity which had generally been attached to 'other ranks' up to that time. The Thompson Trio's 'royal' booking at Aldershot had been arranged by their agents at this time, Macdermott and Holmes. Amusingly this was the Macdermott who sang the sensational 'Jingo' song in 1877:

> We don't want to fight, but by Jingo if we do,
> We've got the ships, we've got the men, we've got the money too!
> We've fought the Bear before, and while we're Britons true
> The Russians shall not have Constantinople.

Whilst a thousand comic singers, male and female, in a thousand music halls, trumpeted their pride in the mother country's imperial progress overseas, they were acutely aware of the dreary lives of the inarticulate masses at home. A life of hard work, if there was work; a life where pity was the exception rather than the rule. A life governed by the weekly visit to the pawnbroker, and by the debt collector. William Ross and Alfred Bowker's song in that Broadhead's penny song sheet has some telling lines:

> I'm an auctioneer of experience wide
> At selling any article,
> Which I get knock'd down to the highest bid,
> Of pity I've not a particle,
> The old dame here she kept a school,
> But the school it wouldn't keep her,
> And the furniture I've got to sell,
> Before she in debt gets deeper.
> So who'll give a bid for the three pot eggs,
> The clock without works, and the chair without legs,
> A summons for rent, and a lot of clothes pegs
> Now who'll be the highest bidder.

But W. H. Broadhead & Son were builders rather than bidders, and to the ten theatres held when Willie died they were to add eight more theatres and places of amusement. At Morecambe, however, the Broadheads bid for and secured the Winter Gardens and its surrounding properties for £20,000 at the time of a small-pox scare.

Successful businessman though he may have been, W. H. Broadhead was also a proud family man, and at holiday times the family home 'Seafield' would be bursting at the seams with grandchildren:

> We helped him when we stayed at Seafield to open the mail which came from the theatres every morning – the box office returns, always in the same type of envelope printed in bold black letters; and the paper knife was handed to the grand-daughter or grand-son staying there, and seventeen envelopes were slit open most meticulously. 'It is very important' Grandpa said, 'To open them cleanly'. So we did. We became very proficient with his paper-knife.

GEO. MOZART.

George Mozart as Colonel Nutty

Birmingham Empire poster

His entertainment interests had grown far beyond the modest beginnings at the Baths, where his wife Mary took her turn in the paybox, and his daughters Nan and Kitty 'used to take the coppers home in buckets' to be counted. Money is still counted on this site, because the Baths were replaced by the Alhambra, then the Palace and finally Lewis's Stores.

Between 1888 and 1894, Percy Honri carefully entered all the Trio's engagements into a narrow black leather book, including their visits to the continental halls and, in 1893, to the American vaudeville houses, in his characteristic hand writing. Besides the many return bookings at music halls, the Trio would work circus or at the exotic Royal Aquarium which used to be where the Central Hall, Westminster, is now. It boasted that 'doors open at noon, and close at 11.30 p.m.' and offered a strange mixture of freak show, circus, aquashow, concert hall and music hall. Sometimes Dezano – 'the Man Serpent' and Fred Paulsen – 'the American Hercules' shared the bill with the 'Elastic Revels and Burlesque Absurdities' of the Haytors, Servais Le Roy – 'the most accomplished Sleight of Hand Exponent in the World', Succi – 'the Fasting Man' who is 'fasting for forty days – holds receptions all day long at West End Entertainment Court' and 'Professor Beckwith's Aquatic Entertainments'. Admission was one shilling; children were half-price, but were admitted free under the age of eight.

In circus, the Thompson Trio used to work from time to time with the Livermore Bros Court Minstrels, who worked in the traditional Christy Minstrel style except that they wore full-bottomed wigs and authentic court dress of George II with their 'burnt cork' make-up. They played a season with the Livermores at Christmas 1892, where one of the 'cornermen' was a musical eccentric, Dave Gillings, who fancied branching out into music hall and decided to team up with 'Posh' West, a bass player in the Livermore band. Harry Thompson suggested that they might like to use some 'Virto & Thompson' routines, and gave them a name for the act 'Engist & Horsa – the most legitimate Funny Musical Act extant'. He fixed their first date, too, at the Alexandra, Wigan. Later Gillings took another partner, a clever tenor and pianist called Charles Warrington, to form a musical act 'Warrington & Gillings'. They had a number of bookings under that name, but Oswald Stoll advised them that the names were awkward to bill outside the Parthenon.

'You want to try a single name. . .'

'How about Mozart, Mr Stoll?'

That was how 'Mozart' came to be billed outside Stoll's music hall in Liverpool, and Dave Gillings became George Mozart – 'the Musical Comedian' and a life-long friend of Percy Honri and his parents. Music hall folk always stuck together.

In his book *Limelight*, George Mozart tells of an amusing time when, as 'The Mozarts', he and his partner bluffed a date at Collins' Music Hall with the help of a friendly cabbie when they had 'just threepence between us'. They heard that a double act was required by 'The Chapel on the Green' for Easter Monday, so they decided to walk from York Road to Islington Green. About a hundred yards from the music hall, they recognised Herbert Sprake and Teddy Barnes, the proprietor and his manager:

FROM THE Prince of Wales
Aquatic Theatre & Baths,
BLACKPOOL.
W. H. BROADHEAD, MANAGER.

GRAND
PERFORMANCES
DAILY
DURING THE
SEASON.

The Royal Thompson Trio
Blackpool.

On this your 84th performance
this Season and third engagement
with me. Your show goes
brighter & fresher than ever.
I much regret your engagements
prevent you staying all the season
Let me have your first vacant
date and oblige
Yours truly
W H Broadhead.

Top left, Percy and Nan after
their marriage; above,
congratulatory letter and original
envelope, 1896; left, Blackpool
excursion trains 1896 © *British Rail*

My partner suddenly had an inspiration . . . and I proceeded to carry out his instructions to the letter. . . .

'Cabbie, you see those couple of swells standing near Collins'?'

'Yes, guv . . . the little one had me chucked out last Saturday after I'd spent a couple of bob on the rotten beer . . . running the 'all too la-de-da-de, no wonder they call it a chapel. . . .'

'Look here . . . we're a couple of pros a bit hard up. Will you drive us up there where they're standing for threepence? We want to make a great impression on them — see what I mean?'

'Jump in . . . keep your coppers, cocky, I've got ye, when I pull up give me a penny. I'll make out it's half-a-dollar, leave it to me — good luck.'

We took him at his word, jumped in the cab — and in less than half a minute were in front of Collins' Music Hall.

'How much?'

'One and sixpence . . . Blimey, it's half a dollar. You're a toff, thank you gentlemen' and drove off back to the rank.

. . . We had created a good impression. My partner walked up to Sprake and presented our business card.

'We are the Mozarts. I take it you are the boss here? Well, we have just arrived from Australia. You want a turn for Monday — well, here we are!'

We were invited upstairs to the office, and came away with a contract at a joint salary of £6 per week for two weeks certain. It was a godsend to us. . . .'

George never tells us whether the Mozarts paid the cabbie commission on the engagement. There are many stories about out-of-work pros, but my favourite one also concerns Collins'.

A little comic is sitting in his attic room in Brixton. He hasn't a date in the book and owes for the letty. A wire comes from Lew Lake at Collins': COMIC SICK WORK TONIGHT. Our hero decides that if he starts walking now, he'll reach Islington for first house; quickly he wraps his props up in brown paper and string, having carefully chalked the collars and studholes on his dickyfront. It's a long walk to Islington, and he's looking forward to getting an advance so that he can have a square meal before doing his turn.

'Good evening, Mr Lake. Thanks for the wire. Where do I put my props?'

'Don't need you after all, Charlie. The big turn's fit. Sorry about that. Perhaps you never got my second wire?'

'That's alright, Mr Lake. Some other time maybe. . .?'

With great dignity the little comic starts to walk back to Brixton. With the dusk that has now fallen comes a gentle drizzle, and he turns up the collar of his thin jacket. The rain gets harder, and the brown paper around his props is gradually disintegrating. He reaches Effra Road, the weather seems to have driven everyone indoors, except for one lady in a doorway. She is enormous, befurred, and heavily made-up. Mechanically she calls out to the bedraggled comic:

TEL. GER. 0612

Willy Clarkson

I promise to give your enquiries re Costumes, Wigs, Masks, etc., my best attention at all times.

For and on behalf of
WILLY CLARKSON
41 – 3, WARDOUR ST, W.I.

Wigs

Far left, Willy Clarkson 'prop. fiver'; Percy Honri as, left, the Jolly Jester and below left as Stage Doorkeeper; below, Jester Costume design

STAGE DOOR

'Good night, cheeky!'

SOLO TURN

Most weeks *The Stage* carries a modest advert on the lines: 'Thanks to Charlie Farnsbarnes Esq. for enquiry. Arrangements completed.' Or there's a star name who books a full page to announce he has 'broken the box office record for the fourth successive time!'. In the halcyon days of music hall, proprietors' recommendations were sparingly given, and so naturally eagerly used by performers to advertise their talents. I found a number of Percy Honri's American commendations, including this one from W. H. Broadhead dated 25 July 1896, complete with its envelope. Why did Percy preserve this particular note? Was it perhaps because Nan had delivered it? – Miss Annie Broadhead whom he had known since she was a little girl, and with whom he had fallen in love? But Percy is a proud man and realises that the junior member of a musical trio is hardly a catch for the daughter of one of Blackpool's leading families.

'I have got to be an established performer in my own right, before we can marry; but the Trio have at least two years' work in the book, and Tony Pastor wants us back in New York.' He rehearses a speech to himself as he heads for George Gettins', the tailor's in Church Street. Percy's offstage appearance is quite dandified, and on previous visits to Blackpool he had added to his wardrobe with one of Mr Gettins' suits. His favourite style is one he adopted when the Trio were in New York three years earlier, and his new suit is to be similar in silver grey.

'Yes, it did us good that American tour – and our "Star Vaudeville Company" idea has been a moneymaker – featured billing, but it's still the "Royal Thompson Trio with Percy Honri".'

The dummy in the window of 'George M. Gettins – stylish tailoring' seems to smirk at him as he enters the shop.

'That reminds me, I owe Professor Vox a letter – gread and gutter . . . gottle of geer"!'

'Good morning, Mr Honri – your suit is ready. Please step inside and I will pack it up for you. Perhaps you want to try it on again? . . .' Mr Gettins burbles on with comments on the watershow, and the increased crowds since the Tower was opened. Percy decides to talk over his plans with his parents that evening.

The Thompsons get on well together, and every night after the show they unwind over Mrs Ashworth's suppers. Most times they cater for themselves, but at Blackpool they relax. The Castle Inn in Market Street is their Blackpool base, and they always stay here. Mrs Ashworth enjoys having pros and hearing all the gossip of the halls. Nearly every town has at least one music hall, and these spawn other services – a host of lodgings who 'take in' and tell you 'Tis at bottom oft' yard an' durn't pull t'string or yo'll let Pa's pigeons out!' The 'Mas' who don't take 'theatricals reg'lar like' wait for the Sunday trains to arrive with the No. One and No. Two Touring Companies with their individual company label stuck on the window of the reserved compartment. Many a pro who hasn't booked digs will judge the assembled landladies at the ticket barrier by the whiteness of their aprons.

Variety folk adapt themselves easily to the tempo of a town; their performances are scaled to this as well to the size of the theatre and the orchestra; the Royal Aquarium boasts fifty musicians, but who can carry that number of band books? — or they could be using a scratch band hastily assembled via an advert in *The Era*:

> Wanted Trumpet. Must be clean shirted. Characters save stamps. Apply M. D. Jagg's Varieties.

They have organised for themselves a world of their own which centres around 'the act'. In London, the Brixton—Kennington area is already established as the pros' home base within easy reach of the forty-one London music halls.

We are now a long way from the days when comedians were still performing at the song and supper rooms for 'three half-crowns per night and two hot drinks'. Just the same, that last-minute telegram: 'WIRE LOWEST' would nearly always elicit the wired reply: 'AM COMING'.

But the days of touring for the Trio were numbered. Percy's mother fell ill, and instead of the Trio returning to America as planned, Percy Honri embarked on his career as a solo turn. His parents settled at The Blue Post in Stafford as publicans, the first time for eighteen years they remained in one place for any length of time.

In a lengthy interview one week in *The Era*, Percy recalled his start as a solo turn:

> Like Dick Whittington, I came to London — not with a cat, but with a concertina — and I very soon found that anyone who had made a name in the provinces was not necessarily considered of much account in the Metropolis. My first experience, after tramping about London for a month and almost begging for work, was that I gave a trial before a manager, who, when I had finished, told me to 'go back to the woods'. . . .

However, the same afternoon Grandpa appeared privately before Mr Glenister at the London Pavilion and got an immediate engagement at that hall. He never forgot Frank Glenister of the 'Pav'. That Saturday, 20 May 1899, *The Era* carried the following paragraph: 'Mr Percy Honri, the talented vocalist and concertinist, makes his debut in the London music halls on Monday next (May 22nd) at the London Pavilion and Collins. Mr Honri intends to stay in Europe for twelve months when he will return to America as he is already booked to appear during 1900–1.'

His father had an apt pupil in Percy as far as publicity was concerned. The following Saturday, his debut as a soloist at the 'Pav' evoked the following *Era* comment:

> . . . a refined musical performance by Percy Honri, who plays the concertina like an artist. Several of these instruments are manipulated by the performer whose skill and taste are unquestionable. . . . 'Light Cavalry' brought forth such continued applause that Mr Honri gave us a specimen

Left and bottom left, Percy Honri's London Pavilion adverts in *The Era* 1906 and 1899; below, front cover and inside of Glenister's First Complimentary Matinee programme; right, Percy Honri 1899

LONDON PAVILION,
May 29th, 1899.

LONDON · PAVILION ·
EVERY EVENING AT 9.30
THE WORLDS GREATEST CONCERTINIST
Percy Honri

PERCY HONRI TONIGHT AT 9.30

Programme,

The following Artistes have kindly promised to   appear by permission of their respective Managers.

1 OVERTURE	26 FOX, IMRO	54 MATTEI, SIGNOR TITO
2 AVOLOS, THE GREAT	27 FREEMAN, HARRY	(Pianoforte Solo).
3 BARCLAY, LAWRENCE	28 GANTHONY, NELLIE	55 DUET
4 BARLOW, BILLIE	29 GLENN, ROSA	J. MUNRO COWARD (Mustel Organ)
5 BELLONINI, WALTER	30 GOTHAM QUARTETTE	SIGNOR TITO MATTEI (Pianoforte)
6 BIGNELL, CHARLES	31 GREEN, EVIE	56 M'NAUGHTONS, THE
7 BIONDI, SIGNOR UGO	32 HARWOOD, ROBB	57 MELFORD, MARK
8 BLANCHE, ADA	33 HAYDON, ETHEL	58 MILDARE, CHARLES
9 BRANTFORD, TOM	34 HIGGINS, JOHN	59 MOORE, G. W.
10 BURNAND, LILY	35 HONRI, PERCY	60 MURRAY, SLADE
11 CAMPBELL, HERBERT	36 HURLEY, ALEC	61 NELSTONE & ABBEY
12 CAPPER, CHARLES	37 JAMES, DAISY	62 OLIVE TRIO
13 CASELLI, CORA	38 JAMES, KATE	63 PAULTON, HARRY
14 CHIRGWIN, G. H.	39 LANGTRY, LILY	64 POLUSKIS, THE
15 COLLETTE, MARY	40 LASHWOOD, GEORGE	65 POULTON, A. G.
16 COLLINS, LOTTIE	41 LAW, LENA	66 RAFFERTY, PAT
17 COWARD, J. MUNRO	42 LEAMORE, TOM	67 RANDALL, HARRY
(Mustel Organ).	43 LE HAY, JOHN	68 RAYBURN, KITTEE
Fantasia Pastorale *J. M. Coward.*	44 LENA, LILY	
(a) Introduction and Procession.	45 LENNARD, ARTHUR	
(b) Rustic Dance.	46 LENO, DAN	
(c) The Storm.	47 LESLIE, FANNIE	
(d) Choir and Organ in Distance.	48 LLOYD, ALICE	
(e) The Storm passes. Finale.	49 LLOYD, MARIE	
18 CUTLER, KATE	50 LYNCH, ELINORE G.	
19 DUGGAN, MAGGIE	51 MACKEY, JULIE	
20 ELVIN, JOE	52 MAGGI, SIGNOR	
21 EVANS, WILL	53 MARGUERITE, MLLE.	
22 FABER, ARTHUR		
23 FISHER & LEONI		
24 FORD, HARRY		
25 FORDE, FLORRIE		

69 REEVE, ADA
70 REEVES, Mrs. SIMS
71 ROBEY, GEORGE
72 SELBINIS, THE
73 STANDING, HERBERT
74 STANHOPE, ERROLL
75 STORMONT, LEO
76 STRATTON, EUGENE
77 STUART, LESLIE
78 TATE, HARRY
79 VERNON, HARRIETT
80 VICTORIA, VESTA
81 WENTWORTH, BESSIE
82 WIELAND, CLARA
83 WILLIAMS, BRANSBY
84 WILTON, MARIE
85 ZANETTOS, THE

86   First and probably the last appearance of the

DOO-DA-DAY MINSTRELS,

In which Mr. G. W. MOORE will appear (by permission of the Directors of Moore & Burgess, Limited).

HIS FIRST PUBLIC APPEARANCE SINCE HIS RETIREMENT.

Bones :   Tambos :
Mr. G. W. MOORE.   Interlocutor :   Mr. DAN LENO
Mr. HARRY RANDALL.   Mr. HERBERT CAMPBELL.   Mr. JOE ELVIN
Mr. TOM M'NAUGHTON.   Mr. EUGENE STRATTON
Mr. EUGENE STRATTON will revive "The Whistling Coon."
Messrs. BRANSBY WILLIAMS, ALEC HURLEY, HARRY TATE, FRED M'NAUGHTON, WALTER LAWLEY, PAT RAFFERTY, WALTER BELLONINI, GEORGE LASHWOOD, CHARLES MILDARE, HARRY FREEMAN and BEN BROWN.

🎵 **NATIONAL ANTHEM.** 🎵

Pianoforte kindly lent by Messrs. Pleyel Wolff & Co.
Mustel Organ kindly lent by Messrs. Metzler & Co.

of his vocal powers by singing 'Because I love you' in which he displayed a cultivated method. . . .

And at Collins', where he doubled, '. . . the concertina used to be regarded as an instrument of torture by peaceable inhabitants of the London suburbs, but musical taste and culture have changed all that, and Mr Percy Honri who is positively a virtuoso gets most charming effects. . . .'

He made a quick return to the 'Pav': 'His turn is certainly one of the best things in the 'Pav' bill . . .', and later at Swansea Empire he '. . . came in for an excellent reception for his manipulation of varied musical instruments, particularly the concertina. This artiste is only young, but he is already in the front rank of his class, and seems like getting to the very top.'

'I am working by myself now, and booked up for twelve months; go to America in November and open at the Union Square Theatre, New York, after which I tour the States till Easter. I play things that have never been attempted before by any concertina player, and do nearly every standard overture published' he said in an interview for the *Cambria Daily Leader*, 4 August 1898. On 6 August his agent Tom Pacey took a full page in *The Era* to announce: 'Percy Honri – the World's Greatest Concertinist.'

Before he went to America, he worked a bill at Gatti's, Charing Cross, on which Katie Lawrence, who originated the immortal *Daisy bell*, was playing. Percy played *The lost chord* and did 'full justice to this ever welcome composition, the sweet melody of which delights even the most unmusical of people. Mr Honri's turn is an agreeable variation from the ordinary round of song and dance.' In 1966, I played the same tune on the very same stage 'under-the-arches', because Gatti's, Charing Cross, is now famous as the Players Theatre.

THE POWER OF MUSIC

Every music hall had an atmosphere of its own – different music halls attracted different patrons; and comics who'd stormed them at the Paragon or the Euston might receive a lukewarm reception at the Alhambra or the Tivoli. Mentioning the Paragon reminds me of one of Grandpa's stories:

'I was playing *Tannhauser* that week – the Overture that is – and remember the Paragon is a huge music hall in the Mile End Road. It held well over four thousand when it was full, and that night it was full of honest to goodness cloth-capped cockneys. But wonderfully quiet, and listening to the chords on the concertina. You could have heard a pin drop during the double-piano passages. Then I heard it – a rumbling and tinkling. It was dozens and dozens of beer bottles rolling down from the back of the pit, and landing up in piles by the band. So before I went into my next number, I invited my new musical arrangers Bass and Guinness to count their bars again. . . .'

In the seventeenth century, Congreve might have been able to write that 'music hath charms to sooth a savage breast', but at the birth of the twentieth century Percy soon realised the power of music, and was determined that his concertina would always remain the feature of the programme'. *The Power of Music* was the name he gave his new act, and here were the seeds of *Concordia* that was to reappear in various forms up to the outbreak of the 1914 war. The earliest version in a musical sense was presented during his American tour of '98 and '99, but he felt that there was a need for a plot, a developing theme. His agent Tom Pacey liked the idea, and suggested that Cecil Newton was experienced in writing sketches and that sort of thing and could write Percy a musical monologue. The sketch has always been a feature of music halls, and Joe Elvin and George Gray were two prominent exponents of that theatre-form. Wal Pink usually wrote Joe's scripts, which often had a racing theme. *Toffy's trotter*, *Over the sticks* and *On the flat* evoke the sporting affinity between the halls and the turf; whilst George Gray's series of 'Fighting Parson's sketches ensured that both Canterbury and Queensberry could gain applause.

Slipped in one of Grandpa's scrapbooks I found Cecil Newton's draft for *The Power of Music* dated 23 August 1899, scribbled in longhand over eleven pages torn from a penny exercise book. It is a curious script which turns rather obviously on the unseen wife and unseen maid sharing the same name! Its quaintness makes it worth quoting at length, because it gives some insight into the style of dialogue that music hall audiences expected to hear at the turn of the century. There is only one character, a composer, Cyril Otway, who has completed a comic opera which he acts out for us with illustrations on his favourite concertina:

> As curtain rises Cyril enters in evening dress, overcoat, opera hat etc. He removes coat and hat, throws himself into a chair by the fireplace.
>
> 'What a jolly time I have had, a grass widower for a month and this is the last day of my liberty. I wonder what my wife will say when she hears that my new comic opera has been accepted. I can hardly believe that I, Cyril Otway, am a fully fledged author and composer.
>
> 'By jove, I could do with a whisky and soda. Where's Clara? Clara — Clara! She's gone to bed; it's deuced awkward having a servant with the same name as your wife — you see when the neighbours hear me cursing the servant — and I do that pretty often — they think I'm cursing my wife!
>
> 'Yes, I've written an opera at least a comic opera, well it isn't exactly comic and it isn't exactly an opera, but, well, I call it a comic opera. I'll describe it to you:
>
> 'There's a Juvenile Man, when I say juvenile, don't think he's young because most juvenile men are old, on the stage, and there's a Heavy Man, well to tell the truth literally, he's not a heavy man, he weighs about eight stone when he's had his hair cut. But he's very wicked, you see most Heavy Men are wicked, and then:
>
> 'There's a Chambermaid — she's called the Chambermaid, but never does any work, she just fools around with a feather brush and short skirts. Chambermaids always wear short skirts and a perpetual smile and of course something else!
>
> 'Then there's the Butler but he's always called the faithful retainer. I suppose they call him that because he faithfully retains everything he can get hold of.

The prototypes of Cecil Newton's *Power of Music* characters? Leading Lady and the Heavy Man (The Blessings), Low Comedian, Butler and Juvenile Man, Chambermaid (May Sherrard)

'Lastly there's the Leading Lady, oh she's not really the leading lady, the Heavy Man does all the leading.

'The scene opens, and the villagers, at a shilling a night, are discovered drinking a copious draught of nothing from a pasteboard pot. They sing:

> We'll shout, hooray, hooray
> The master comes home today
> Today, today. Hooray, Hooray, Hooray.

And when they get well on in the Chorus you can't tell the 'todays' from the 'hoorays'. After they've finished they sidle off.

'Then on comes the Juvenile Man. The church bells ring, and he begins to sing. There's poetry for you!

> Come to my arms, my lady fair
> How long I have sought for thee
> How can I ever tell the world
> All that thou art to me.

'On the last "art to me" he goes off, and the Leading Lady accompanied by the remains of his music comes on like this:

> Oh would I were a moth
> That I might fly to he
> To whom I plight my troth
> For I would fly with thee.

At the last rehearsal she sang: "Oh would I were a moth-er." Of course that didn't sound nice. On comes the heavy light man and takes her by surprise, that is by her hand:

> At last I find the maiden fair
> And offer thee my hand.
> Before I take thee to my lair
> In a far-off foreign land.

'Enter the Juvenile Man — a chord: Why what is this?
Leading lady: He hath insulted me.
Heavy Man: I say 'tis false.
Juvenile Man: Oh is this true?
Heavy man: She is my mistress.
Juvenile man: I say you lie man.
Heavy man: You cannot prove it.
Low Comedian: Oh, no but I can — Chord!!
Entrance of Chorus: Ha, Ha, our mistress now is free, Ha Ha, Ha Ha, Ha Ha, Ha Ha.
On the last Ha Ha curtain falls. End of act. Play selection on concertina.'
Cyril Otway then rises, and takes letter from mantelpiece, and opens it:

'It looks like my wife's writing – great Heavens! What's this! "I have left you for ever. Do not ask the reason why or ever attempt to search for me, I have gone to one whose object in life will be to make happiness the existence of your unhappy – Clara."'

He drops the letter: 'A few moments ago I stood on the threshold of a happy career, now I can only look forward to a ruined life. How all the past comes back to me – I see myself a happy bridegroom marching up the aisle – even the tune the sweet organ pealed forth comes back to me.' (Organ selection) 'Her favourite song seems dinning in my ears – I'll sing it tonight for the last time.' (Song and Business)

'Well my dream of life is over, but I must start afresh, broken hearts are not in favour with the world – life is only a masquerade after all. But I must destroy this letter. Why, what on earth is this? "Dear Sir, The letter on the other page was copied from 'The Young Ladies Bliss' by a friend of mine, h'as it h'expresses my sentiment exactly. I forfeit my month's wages and 'opes this finds you has it leaves me. Clara Jenkins. P.S. I didn't mind yer ways, but I couldn't stand yer moosic."'

'Hooray, Clara my wife, forgive me – my happiness is restored. I am rid of a veritable terror – the slavey. Ah great indeed is the Power of Music.' (Selection and Curtain)

Cecil Newton Aug 2 3 '99.

Newton posts the draft direct to Percy Honri who has good billing at the Lyric, Bath. The programme includes a family act of harpists and banjoists, the Henderson & Stanley Quartet, who include comedy acrobatics as well in their turn. The manager Harry Williams has engaged a strong bill that week: Sisters Irving – 'Variety Dancers'; Fred Elson – 'Character Comedian'; Emma Don – 'Male Impersonator'; Josephine Henley who is 'the possessor of a fine voice, which she uses with skill in comic song and ballad'; Morris and Morris – 'American grotesques' whose turn 'is unique in its own particular line and never fails to create uproarious merriment; Stephenson, the Irish comedian, works with refreshing vigour and his step dancing and patter are both on approved lines'. The Bath critic remembers the band too, with the comment that they 'have plenty to do, and come out of the ordeal with credit'.

A close examination of the scrapbooks seems to confirm that Cecil Newton's *The Power of Music* was never used in the form submitted, but the idea of working in a set appealed to Percy's sense of theatre. More practically the Royal Thompson Trio still had some of the 'fit up' they had used with their 'Star Vaudeville Company'. A postcard went off to Harry Thompson at the Lyceum, Stafford:

'*Power of Music* needs part of drawing-room set to include fireplace and mantlepiece. Need the screen for quick-changes on stage. . . .'

There were no touring problems with stage settings in those days; rail cartage was cheap and the hallkeeper arranged for the skips, cloths and set-pieces to arrive

Right, self-portrait of Dan Leno
© *Trustees of the National Portrait
Gallery*; below, cartoon of Leno
as 'The Shopwalker' from song
cover; Dan and Mrs Leno's
drawing room, Springfield
House, Clapham 1902

George Robey

in good order. If you advertised 'scenic effects carried' that was the cachet of the established performers who would supply their own pictorial posters to supplement the normal theatre bills with their stereotyped layouts.

Using his own new letterheads, Percy wrote to Harrison's to design and make a series of jester motleys of varying hues, and appointments were made for fittings for a whole range of costumes all equipped with cord-releases for the quick changes. He arranged with Cuthbert Clark to make new arrangements of his music, and wired Pacey that he had a new act and wanted bookings for it.

'Now to work on that script – a composer of comic opera with a skivvy named Clara! There'll be no maid – and no comic opera either; and there's far too much patter. It's the power of music not the power of speech. I'll make the hero an M.P. – you need to be a hero to be one these days – he sits in front of the fire with his concertina. He plays *Star of Eve* – that always goes well, and then he dozes off. The rest is his dream – a musical fantasy. In the dream, he sees the letter from his wife on the mantlepiece, and reads the contents as in Newton's draft. However he is determined to find his wife, searches for her in 'Frivolity Hall' disguised as a jester, becomes a coster in Hoxton and tries to find her there, and finally ends up amongst the Montagues and Capulets of Shakespeare's *Romeo and Juliet*. A challenge to fight a duel awakens him, and he sees the letter, reads it and finds that she has gone to the theatre with her parents, and is due back at eleven o'clock. The clock strikes the hour, there's a rat-tat-tat on the door – cue for a rousing chorus song. . . .' Grandpa must have realised that this act would be a turning point for him in his career as a solo performer.

He decided that he would wait until the whole piece was perfect. It was essential to maintain a continuity, and the costume changes needed endless rehearsals. Week by week as he went from town to town, he would add one or other of the new characters he had decided on. The jolly jester came first, and he included the gag of his father where the tiny concertina was concealed in the jester's huge bow tie – he would make as if to adjust the bow, and play *Pop goes the weasel*. It was part of a tried and trusted routine.

The protean actor was well known on the halls. Names like R. A. Roberts and Bransby Williams recall true actors of the halls – for them, the act never stood still, it was in constant flux. But the protean musical act was a distinct novelty and managers booked novelties. There were 267 music halls needing new turns, new novelties every week, 41 of which were in London.

In the autumn of 1901, there is a telegram for him with the stage door keeper. It's from the Trio's old agent, now known as Warner & Co of Wellington Street, Strand, W.C.: 'CAN CONFIRM PAVILION AND COLLINS. . . .' Now the pressure was on for Londoners to see his new act and he would be working with old friends, Dan Leno, George Robey, the Poluskis – remember the children's show they had done together at Brixton on the old Queen's Golden Jubilee. . . .

Dan Leno is topping, naturally. It is a still dazed Dan who barely a week earlier had performed a personal Command Performance for the new King Edward. *The*

Percy Honri 'conducting';
souvenir of Sousa's visit,
6 December 1901; Percy
Honri 1899

Sunday Times had a number of paragraphs on the subject under the heading 'Meditations in Music Halls':

> There has been much to ponder on during the last fortnight, for the oft-asked question 'Can music halls be taken seriously?' has certainly been answered by His Majesty the King, who in commanding a variety artist to Sandringham, did not desire mere prettiness and mediocrity, but singled out one who was positively born in the profession and made his debut at the early age of three, and who, by sheer hard work and determination, has worked his way to the first place on the variety stage, and is unspoilt by success. The great compliment paid by the King to Mr Dan Leno is appreciated by all his admirers, and should encourage those who cater for the amusement of the public.
>
> Until the pantomime draws closer, visitors to the London Pavilion will have the opportunity of hearing two of the best songs Dr Dan Leno has yet had – 'Buying a House' and 'The Fireman'. They will also enjoy his inimitable dancing and shriek with laughter at his patter, for his turn runs into forty minutes, and the audience laughs the whole time.
>
> Certainly the men are best just now in the programme at the Pavilion. Mr Percy Honri plays the concertina to distraction, and equally well whether clad in evening dress, as a Jester or as Romeo. Costume does not seem to affect his talent. . . . Mr George Robey still impersonates 'Clarence, the last of the dandies', he has never had a better song; and Kelly and Gillette in their Billiard Table act are as amusing and energetic as ever. Here, too, are the Poluskis and the Zanettos. In fact, an excellent entertainment is provided, and the house is crowded every night.

Earlier *The Era*, after adding its tribute to Dan Leno who, 'with his blushing honours thick upon him, returned to receive a welcome that in spontaneous heartiness, warmth and affection could not have been excelled', went on to describe the return of Percy Honri with

> . . . a plan for presenting his act that gives it a most refreshing touch of novelty. As soon as No. 11 is brought to view we hear the strains of his favourite instrument playing a fascinating melody, which he begins to sing in tones of much sweetness as soon as the tableau curtains part, and we discover in him a vocalist of considerable culture. He then makes a quick-change to the character of a jester – a Touchstone – and very appropriately recites the lines 'The man that hath no music in himself' from *The Merchant of Venice*, giving afterwards some imitations of the music of the church organ, and the skirl of the pibroch, choosing the well-known air *The Cock of the North* played by the brave Highland pipers at the glorious charge at Dargai. Another change and Percy becomes the more prosaic coster in pearlies, as he appears at Hampstead on Bank holidays. He complains of his mate's in-

aptitude in a duet, and shows that he has a decided sense of humour. We think this impersonation might be developed with advantage by the young artiste, when, to use professional parlance, he feels himself more in the character. He concludes one of the brightest and most interesting turns we have seen by donning a rich and handsome dress – such as Orsino might have worn. . . . He looks particularly well in this courtier costume, putting the finishing touch to a pronounced success.

As his own publicity put it: '"The Power of Music" [is] constructed to immediately please both the eye and ear.'

Percy Honri had arrived – and he set about consolidating that success. Sousa heard him play, and asked for him at the 'Supper given in honor of John Philip Sousa and his Band' at Oddenino's on 6 December 1901. Sousa invited him to join his band's world tour as the featured guest artist. Grandpa declined, saying that he had bookings that could not be changed. Certainly he would have wanted to go, but it would mean an eighteen-month absence, and he had a booking set for Manchester Cathedral the following December. But Percy never forgot John Philip Sousa or his rousing music, and by 1910 had established the idea of a silver band on stage.

CONCORDIA

On 3 December 1902, Percy married his beloved Nan by special licence in Manchester Cathedral. After their marriage, Percy and Nan took an apartment in Lavender Sweep, Clapham. His concertina was in constant demand, not only in music halls but on the concert platform, including recitals at the Wigmore Hall and Crystal Palace, and many 'after dinner' engagements too. He would say: 'If I can find somewhere to stand, I can give a show.' The music hall circuits wanted his act now, and *The Power of Music* developed into the first edition of his most famous musical sketch – *Concordia*.

In 1959, six years after Grandpa died, my father Baynham Honri decided to use a small legacy to finance his own show, which we wrote and I directed for the summer season at Exmouth in South Devon. We knew the area well, having been there during the war, and the bandstand in the manor grounds was where I had appeared with Wally Watson's 'Cosmopolitan Follies' eleven years earlier. It was a well-known concert party pitch, the 'Follies' had been an Exmouth fixture for many seasons. We decided to call our show *Concordia Follies* – 'Concordia' after Grandpa's production, and 'Follies' to keep up the Exmouth concert party tradition. Although seats were only 3s and 2s, and there were four editions, my father and I were determined that our show would give value for money.

The very day we commenced rehearsals, 8 June 1959, my wife June Bernice presented me with our first child, Sarah Anne Jane. Sarah met her first audience three weeks later. When we returned for the 1960 season, June was singing and dancing with us. With Baynham Honri's electronic expertise the bandstand was transformed into the 'Marquee Theatre' bulging with gadgetry. Two tab tracks

Baynham Honri presents
THE LITTLE BIG SHOW

CONCORDIA FOLLIES

HARRY MARSH · PETER HONRI
JESSICA LYNWOOD · JASMINE BLAIR · KAY BUTLER
BARRY McDONALD · MARGARET WHITE
DEVISED AND DIRECTED BY PETER HONRI

MATINEES 3 P.M. ┃ EVENINGS 7·45
ALL SEATS 2/-   ADMISSION 3/- AND 2/-
CHILDREN HALF PRICE ALL PERFORMANCES.
FOUR EDITIONS · CHANGING TUESDAYS & FRIDAYS

MARQUEE
MANOR GROUNDS   EXMOUTH

Concordia follies 1959: top right, poster; top left, Harry Marsh
and Jessica Lynwood; above, Peter Honri; right, Harry Marsh

Percy Honri IN "CONCORDIA."

5436. ENERGIE

Nᵒ 6187   LONDON,   19

National Provincial Bank Limited

HOLLOWAY BRANCH.
45, SEVEN SISTERS ROAD, LONDON, N.7.

TWO PENCE

Concordia: top right, detail from special cheque; right, pictorial poster hoarding at Bury; below, advance publicity; below right, Percy Honri: 'The Dreamer'

THE DAILY TELEGRAPH.

LONDON, SATURDAY, FEBRUARY 6. *1909*

Step by step the music-hall sketch advances along the path of evolution. Starting in quite a small way, it has rapidly grown in significance and importance, thus bringing the variety and regular theatres into closer and still closer touch. A drama covering the area of five acts is generally considered to be a fairly ample entertainment; relatively, however, it pales its ineffectual fires before a sketch containing eight scenes. That is what is promised by Mr. Blyth-Pratt at the Oxford next Monday week. The novelty, described as a "musical fantasy," bears the name of "Concordia." It is, we are assured, "a wonderful admixture of bright and catchy airs, of sad music, of dainty girls, of graceful dancing, of wild hilarity, of scenes of brilliancy constituting a veritable feast of colour, and of a constant succession of weird happenings, surprising transformations, and quick changes."

were put in, and a saturable reactor dimmer control lighting system installed. Sketches used stereo tape effects, and my father invented a novel musical effect 'pianoflex' so that our pianist Margaret White could play short concerto arrangements with orchestral backing – an arrangement of the '1812' Overture with Moscow burning being particularly effective! Naturally there were teething problems, and I still recall with a shudder the 'front runners' opening behind my announcement for Margaret's solo spot, to find the slapstick sketch props still littering the stage. That particular stage 'damager' tactfully resigned due to 'nerves'.

The West Country press were constructive: '. . . a jolly little revue . . . with several attractive new angles, but I am glad that director Peter Honri has not too harshly changed the pattern of "the summer show" for it was still some of the old fashioned routines I enjoyed the most' wrote Peter Jarman in the *Express & Echo*. *The Stage* added a cautionary comment: '. . . there is, however, a danger that these brilliant technical improvements might trend to overshadow the performers, for to the layman they signify little . . . .' But this is a constant problem with any kind of live presentation – the balance between the electronic and the histrionic.

If the original *Concordia* of 1906 had no hi-fi magnetic tape effects it did include revolving scenery and a film sequence. In a week when Fred Ginnett and Company were appearing in *Turpin's Ride to York* complete with 'the fine mare Black Bess' and Florrie Forde at the Empress, Brixton, Percy Honri's company, now seven strong, was preparing to launch his 'tuneful fantasy', *Concordia*, at Collins' Music Hall, Monday 19 March 1906. I can imagine how carefully the damp, flaky, whitewashed walls of the dungeon-like dressing rooms would have been hung with cotton sheetings to preserve the freshness of the costumes. There were six sets of each costume worn by Percy and his assistants. Each set was of a different colour so that each day's audience would see the fantasy in a different hue, and *The Encore*, after giving a resùme of the plot, concludes with the prophetic comment: '. . . This pretty fantasy is splendidly staged and acted, and meets with very hearty approval, and should have a very successful career before it. . . .' It did; Percy Honri played it in various guises for twelve years!

HAVE YOU SEEN 'CONCORDIA'?

So delightfully played by Percy Honri, with the able assistance of a Clever Company of Comedians and Beautiful Girls who introduce in a 30-minute act more original notions than any ten shows at present buying railway tickets. In a lightning's flash Percy Honri portrays the 'Dreamer' with his dalliance of delusive distraction – the 'Coster' with his Caricaturing Cockneys – the 'Jester' with his Jingle of Jollificating Joviality – the 'Mephisto' with his Mete of Mutinous Melody – the 'Cinnocoon' with his Circumlocution of Cupiditious Coruscate. The performance is scened by Hemsley. Costumed by Harrison Ltd. Cinemato'd by Urban, Pictorialized by Staffords. Thought of by Percy Honri. Admired by Everyone.

Every music hall manager and agent in the country received that message in a special 1907 New Year card; a year in which there would be great advances made by performers. Grandpa's publicity blurb ends with the words 'Admired by Everyone' – over sixty years later I meet people who remember *Concordia* vividly. Perhaps they were in that Monday first house audience at Swindon Empire, 25 May 1908, when it 'evoked a furore quite beyond what has been accorded anything else within recent memory . . . it appeals so strongly to the imagination as almost to obliterate everything else from the subsequent impressions of the evening's entertainment'. In June 1962, I had a charming letter from the eighty-four year old actor-manager Percy Court, who wrote: 'I can say that *Concordia* was a really lovely show full of incidents and surprises in changing the scenery, having built it on what was known in those days as a "revolve". The whole of the cast was about 30 and it was beautifully dressed – a really lovely show. . . .'

Jess Sweet wrote to my father at Ealing Studios in October 1955 these recollections of working as stage director on the 1907 version of the show:

> I can well remember spending days on end with him before the production [at the Holloway Empire] working out the intricate practicalities of the revolving scenery which was its great novelty. Even now I can remember all the details, and have often thought the same principles could be incorporated in television and film sets at low cost. . . . After several tours of *Concordia*, we did a combination or road show, the first of its kind. This consisted of several variety acts – plus *Concordia* – a troupe of Boy Scouts, billed as 'Percy Honri's Boy Scouts' whom I used to lead in a sort of tattoo and sing the solos – then came Percy Honri's Marionettes, the puppets being worked by your father, myself and your grandfather, Mr Harry Tomps! We certainly had to be versatile in those days. . . .

The company had grown, and so had Grandpa's publicity efforts – in 1910 there was not one week vacant thanks to thirteen consecutive front pages in *The Performer*. That year's *Performer* Annual gave the full cast of *Concordia* as: Messrs Harry Baroux, George Cooper, Albert Lewis, Tom Fetherstone, J. W. Garnett, Tom McKay, A. Millar, George Piercy, Arthus Sinclair, Harry Smallshaw, Frank Tritschler, Robert Burton and the Misses Kitty Albert, Louie Arnold, Margaret Cefu, Ada Cresser, Winifred Lewis, Gertrude Lawson, Lillie Leicester, Jessie Merrick, Violet Tremayne and Gertrude Winter, Quetta Pappucci played the Spirit of Phantasy, and the musical director was Arthur Grimmett.

Kitty Albert who met and married her husband Harry Baroux while on tour with *Concordia* in 1912, recalled her memories of those music hall days for the Christchurch New Zealand paper *Pegasus Post* in 1971: 'Percy Honri was best man and arranged a champagne wedding breakfast for us and the whole cast, but Mrs Honri refused to come to the wedding herself, because she said it brings bad luck if a mother-to-be attends a wedding. But she promised to throw a shoe down the stairs for us, to bring good luck, and this she did. . . .'

Besides her long stay with *Concordia*, Kitty Albert had created a furore as the

Concordia: scenes from 'Frivolity Hall'

THE Palladium

ARGYLL STREET, OXFORD CIRCUS, LONDON, W.
Adjoining Central London and Bakerloo Railways, Oxford Circus Stations.
Chairman - OSWALD STOLL.   Managing Director - WALTER GIBBONS

6.10 TWO PERFORMANCES DAILY 9.10
3 Performances — Mondays, Wednesdays and Saturdays
AT 2.30, 6.10 and 9.10

MONDAY, NOV. 27th, 1911

PERCY HONRI
And his colossal Combine in a new edition of the
GREAT MUSICAL SCENIC PHANTASY
CONCORDIA

On a scale totally eclipsing all previous efforts which justly places PERCY HONRI as the Bleriot of Spectacular Producers,

1—The Dream.   2—Frivolity Hall.   3—A Street in Hoxton
4—The Demon Woods. 5—The Dressing Room. 6—The Man in the Moon. 7—A Musical Allegory. 8—The Awakening.

80 carefully selected Artistes contribute to this Wonderful Act the features of which are the famous Concertina Solos rendered by PERCY HONRI, the Joking Wind Jammer and Inventor (writer and composer of "Concordia"). In a Lightning's Flash Percy Honri portrays The DREAMER, with his dalliance of delusive distraction, the COSTER with his Caricaturing Cockneys, the JESTER with his Jingle of Jollificating Joviality, MEPHISTO with his Metoof Mutinous Medley, the CINACOON with his Circumlocution of Cupiditious Coruscate.

Augmented Orchestra: Conductor ♦ Mr. ARTHUR GRIMMETT.

Concordia: topping the Palladium bill; scenes from 'A Street in Hoxton'

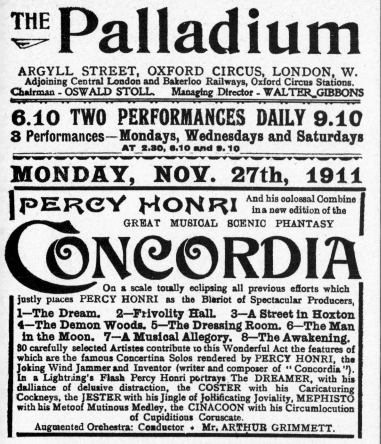

original 'Gibson Girl' in the national tour of the musical comedy *The Prince of Pilsen* — one reviewer wrote 'the famous walk, as illustrated by Miss Kate Albert, brought down the house'. As the *Pegasus Post* puts it 'in the good old days of Vaudeville when the theatres and music halls of Harrogate, Wakefield, Birkenhead, Dewsbury, Ramsgate and countless other English country towns resounded to the applause of audiences delighted with the "Yankee bustle" of this colourful show. For the older generations among us, the very name "Gibson Girl" (pronounced "Gel" as of then) is enough to conjure up the outrageous silhouette of feminine beauty immortalised by the celebrated American artist Charles Dana Gibson and personified by Kitty Albert as she was in those days.'

But a show is for an audience, and when *Concordia* was at the Palladium in November 1911, the *Daily Chronicle* had been organising a competition to 'write about your favourite Music Hall turn'. One of the entries came from twenty-four year old Arthur Thorn of Stratford East who had very clear ideas on the impact the show had on him, when he entered the essay competition:

> Concordia — the very name is mystic, indeed it would be no extreme of criticism to label Percy Honri a mystic, he has undoubtedly the rare faculty of 'Sight', and he has handled in his creation 'Concordia' a very difficult subject with remarkable skill. A true psychological treatment of the Spirit of a dream, at least that is how 'Concordia' impressed me. He has splashed a large canvas, not only with the fantastic weaving of the vivid colours of life, but also with them the most bewildering eccentricities conceivable; how true is this to the Nature of a dream? Surprise is the soul of a dream, and surprise is the elusive element fascinating and charming of Percy Honri's 'Concordia'. He has given to the Music Hall public the weirdest dream conceivable accompanied by sweet melody into the very crannies of mystery. West End to East End, East End to Fairyland, Fairyland to the Moon, the Moon back to the West End. His quick changes are so marvellous that one does not pause to consider the fact that he does change, we are intoxicated by the smoothness of the production, the action is uninterrupted. We do not wonder if it really is Percy Honri who passes so dreamily from one contrasted phase to another; his is the 'art that conceals art', and thus the illusion that he sets out to create in the mind of the audience is really an illusion; it is a dream that we are watching, not a mere 'quick-change' performance. A French poet has said that 'we are children when we dream', Percy Honri's 'Concordia' is therefore an appeal to the child within us. The Symbol which he employs to suggest this is the delightful little child who dances her way through the dream, like a radiant thought upon the wings of Romance and Simplicity; Percy Honri is a poet, his 'Concordia' is the most original and poetic sketch upon the Variety Stage.

It is interesting to compare a contemporary audience-comment on *Concordia* with the memories of the two veteran performers. In the pre-jazz age of the Edwardians, music hall had become insular and self-indulgent – a tendency that seems to occur in cycles in the industry: 'What do you expect? It's the talkies/the radio/the television/the 'nudes'/the bingo.' The stage was ready for change – and in the music hall world he knew so well, Grandpa looked beyond banging the imperial drum, and in *Concordia* used those hustling tactics of the American vaudeville and burlesque, where the accent is always on what writers then termed 'quick work'. To this brashness, he brought the Parisian revue-style and the natural soulfulness of the French music hall performers and his own love of the countryside and of beautiful things. Percy Honri was a man of peace, and his show took the name of the Roman goddess of Peace; when the world seemed to tire of peace, so *Concordia* died. Were the names of his succeeding sketches, *Bohemia* and *What About It?*, a portent of the anguish that was to come to so many millions?

MARCH 24
1910
THE
PERFORMER

4th ANNIVERSARY NUMBER

PRICE 2d

CONCORDIA

A Vaudeville Fantasy. Monday Next, HIP., HULL.

"CONCORDIA."

INVENTED, WRITTEN, COMPOSED
BY PERCY HONRI.

Concordia: Performer front cover publicity and two 'Concordians'

PERCY HONRI
—always original

Daily Mail

Daily Net **SALE** Six Times as Large as That of Any Penny London Morning Journal Except **"THE TIMES."**

PERCY HONRI
—always original

MONDAY, AUGUST 2, 1915.   LONDON.   MANCHESTER.   PARIS.   No. 6,031.   ONE HALFPENNY

PERCY HONRI IN HIS 1915 REVUE

THE GREATEST ATTRACTION EVER PRESENTED TO A MUSIC HALL AUDIENCE

PERCY HONRI will shortly visit the leading Provincial Towns.

5   WE'RE ALL SHOWMEN

'RATCATCHER'S DAUGHTER — Take Two. Now boys, take the tempo from Peter; and don't forget you're all supposed to be very tipsy, but not maudlin — and you're not a barbershop quartet. Right, sound is running.' The assistant director nods and Ray Holder cues us in, and 'The Three Cripples' drunken glee club begins to sing:

> Not long ago in Westminster
> There liv'd a ratcatcher's daughter,
> But she didn't quite live in Westminster,
> 'Cause she liv'd t'other side of the water.
> Her father caught rats
> And she sold sprats
> All round and about that quarter;
> And the gentle folks all took off their hats
> To the pretty little ratcatcher's daughter.
> Doodle dee! Doodle Dum!
> Di Dum Doodle Da!
> Doodle dee! Doodle Dum!
> Di Dum Doodle Da! . . .

'Right — cut it! . . . That was fine . . . but we'll go again, a little brighter with the tempo. All right? Let's go then . . . Ratcatcher's Daughter — Take Three . . . sound running!'

> Not long ago in Westminster
> There liv'd a ratcatcher's daughter . . .

The previous day Sir Carol Reed had decided that the scene outside 'The Three Cripples' needed a little background singing by the customers, and so a small group of the 'regular *habitués*' held a short recording session on the adjoining sound-stage. We were making the film version of Lionel Bart's musical *Oliver!* In the film

Peter Honri as the concertina man in Columbia's *Oliver*!

I can be seen from time to time with a concertina – a large black one, or with the tiny concertina which years ago Grandpa had got from Dutch Daly, another concertina player of the early halls and the first treasurer of the music hall trade union, the Variety Artistes Federation. It is this concertina that I play with the buskers band for the *Consider yourself* sequence when Mark Lester and Jack Wild tag along with the buskers Eddie Davies and Charlie Gray. There were a great number of music hall performers working on this film, and for six months we worked hard and we played hard. In traditional style the comics filled in the long delays that are inevitable during filming, especially when making complex musicals – they kept the whole unit amused. There was never a dull moment when you were with Sonny Farrar, Eddie Reindeer, Frank Cowley, Vic Wise, George Clarkson, Toby Lennon and Dickie Martin.

Most of us were involved in the musical sequences, working with the choreographer Onna White, and with the musical supervisor John Green. The concertina seemed to intrigue both Johnny Green and Eric Rogers, the musical associate. The range of my 'mini' concertina was carefully noted for the musical arrangements, and I had my first music session with three of the top British session musicians when we recorded the sound track for the 'buskers band'. Johnny Green was not only a great arranger, he was a superb showman in his own right. His recording sessions were a revelation, peppered with wry comments on phrasing and intonation and on three decades of making Hollywood musicals. I had suggested *Ratcatcher's daughter* as a traditional tune of the period in which *Oliver!* was set.

About 120 years before we sang *Ratcatcher's daughter* at Shepperton Studios, the prince of music hall artistes Sam Cowell was singing it to the *habitués* of Evans' Music and Supper Rooms in King Street, Covent Garden. Evans's Late Joys was a basement grill room much favoured by the man-about-town of the 1840s. Notables such as Dickens, Thackeray and the painter Landseer regularly joined their friends there to hear Cowell and Charles Sloman, and to enjoy Paddy Green's 'steak and chops, stout and ale' by the fireside. Sloman was a noted *improvisatore* with a ready wit for the earthy and the barbed. He was the original of Thackeray's little "Nadab' in his book *Pendennis*. We meet him later at the opening of Wilton's New Music Hall and Supper Rooms in April 1859, when *The Era* commented: ' . . . Mr Charles Sloman, under whose experienced supervision the musical department is placed, assists with his well-known improvisatorial talents.' In July 1870 Charles Sloman died in the Strand Union Workhouse. Ewing Ritchie, a temperance advocate, put it like this in his *Night Side of London* published in 1857 ' . . . I can never pass the Cave of Harmony without thinking of the Comic Singer as I last saw him – in the very flush of health and life, stimulated by wine . . . little dreaming of the workhouse in which he was so soon to beg for room to die.'

Charles Sloman followed a well-tried tradition that probably started in this country with Richard Tarleton who in the late sixteenth century adapted the talents in extemporising developed by the Italian companies who had come to England in the 1570s – the *Commedia del Arte*. Tarleton's special talent was to extemporise in rhyme, as in his *Crow sits on the wall* which ran to over seventeen verses, all ending with the catch-phrase 'Please one and please all'. Here is a Goon-like incident from the posthumous *Tarleton's jests* — How Tarleton deceives the Watch in Fleet Street:

> Tarleton, having bin late at court, and comming homwards throw Fleet Street, he espied the watch, and not knowing how to passe them, hee went very fast, thinking by that meanes to goe unexamined. But the watchman, perceiving that hee shunned them, stept to him and commanded him in the Queene's name to stand. 'Stand!' quoth Tarleton, "let them stand that can: for I cannot." So falling downe as though hee had been drunke, they helpt him up, and so let him passe.

No wonder Shakespeare ribbed his comedians in Hamlet, 'and let those that play your clowns speak no more than is set down for them'.

In his erudite but very readable book *Early Doors*, Harold Scott placed Tarleton among

> . . . the aristocracy of that miscellaneous crowd of performers who belong by tradition to the great wandering theatre of the open air. They find their places in the theatre by virtue of the fact that its 'personnel' — actors of morality and tragedy were in early instances enthusiastic amateurs — was dependent in certain cases upon these performers . . . Their material was handed down by tradition through performances at the fairs, in inn-yards, and such other places of assembly as baiting rings and hall hired for perform-ances . . . .

Richard Tarleton, who died in 1588, was known far and wide as a player of jigs — the jigs were danced by the clown, to his own playing on the tabor and pipe. He could also be called the inventor of the costume of the English clown — he acted in very wide trousers and shoes several sizes too big for him, and an enormous felt hat that he would twist into caricatures of the fashionable of that time.

JOEY

Two hundred years later Joe Grimaldi, the greatest of all clowns, was to epitomise for all time the English clown as a distinct character — and the phrase 'joey-joey' entered the pros' vocabulary to indicate a clowning routine. Joey's love of puns remained with him to the end as he signed himself 'Grim-all-day' — a wry comment on his years as the funniest of men.

One day a doctor not knowing who he was said to him: 'I would recommend you see Grimaldi'.

The patient replied: 'I am Grimaldi.'

'Joseph, farewell, dear funny Joe. We met with mirth — we part in pain. For many a long, long year must go, ere Fun can see thy like again.' In his *Ode to Joseph Grimaldi, Senior* Thomas Hood eulogised the original 'Joey' with many satirical asides at other performers and personages of that time:

HERBERT CAMPBELL

Top left, Herbert Campbell;
left, Dan Leno as 'The Guard'
and as 'Dame Trot' from a song
cover; above, Cruikshank's
etching of Grimaldi's farewell
benefit

Joseph! they say thou'st left the stage
To toddle down the hill of life,
And taste the flannell'd ease of age,
Apart from pantomimic strife –
"Retired" – (for Young would call it so) –
"The world shut out" – in Pleasant Row! . . .

Oh, had it pleas'd the gout to take
The reverend Croly from the stage,
Or Southey, for our quiet's sake,
Or Mr Fletcher, Cupid's sage,
Or damme! namby pamby Poole –
Or any other clown or fool!

Ah, where is now thy rolling head!
Thy winking, reeling, drunken eyes
(As old Catullus would have said)
Thy oven mouth, that swallow'd pies –
Enormous hunger – monstrous drowth –
Thy pockets greedy as thy mouth!

Ah, where thy ears, so often cuff'd –
Thy funny, flapping, filching hands! –
Thy partridge body, always stuff'd
With waifs and strays, and contrabands!
Thy foot – like Berkeley's 'Foote' for why?
'Twas often made to wipe an eye! . . .

This art of caricature is deeply ingrained in the music hall arts: one thinks of Chaplin and Keaton, of Robey and Leybourne, of Sid Field and Tony Hancock, of Dan Leno and Max Wall and, on the distaff side, Marie Lloyd, Jenny Hill, Nellie Wallace, Hetty King and Carol Channing.

Rahere, the jester of Henry II who became the first prior of St Bartholomew, had in 1133 begun the famous St Bartholomew Fair with what I term the 'ABC of Music Hall' – acrobats, balancers and comedians. These ABCs are still used today, especially the comedians. Comedians, drolls, grotesques, comics, clowns, merry andrews – these were and are the very stuff of music hall. On a visit to Jack Speed's White Horse, Fetter Lane, in 1763, George Alexander Stevens gathered material for his book *The Adventures of a Speculist*. He gives us an insight into the 'free and easys' and tells us that even then the tradition of 'working turns' was well established:

> . . . There are a set of people about this town, who, from attending to everything but what they should do, have made themselves masters of some particular tunes or oddities, which are by those who know no better, admired as supernatural qualifications.

These people are invited from Club to Club by the landlords of public houses, to play off their fools tricks to all the guests the publican can jumble together. One plays with a rolling pin upon a salt-box; another grunts like a hog; a third makes this teeth chatter like a monkey; and thus they each have something to make the Million laugh, and put common sense out of countenance.

But here, here they come!... Observing to my companion, that none of these STARS paid as they came in, he told me that the landlord always franked them for the tricks they played to divert his customers. Now 'Silence! Silence!' was bawled out by almost every person in the room, and everybody stood up on the President's rising.... After most deliberately hitting three strokes upon the table with his hammer, he began with telling the company: '... that he had a toast or two to propose, after which Mr GRUNTER should either give them the organ, the broom-stick, a French-horn tune, or a song first ...' and with that 'Comus's Court' began.

THE ORIGINAL MUSIC HALL ACT

When George II gave the royal assent in 1752, the term 'music hall' first appeared on the statute book. 'The Music Hall Act' hoped amongst other things '... to correct as far as may be the Habit of Idleness which is become too general over the whole Kingdom, and is productive of much Mischief and Inconvenience ...'.

The Act set down that from 1 December 1752, 'any House, Room, Garden, or other Place kept for public Dancing, Music, or other public Entertainment of the like Kind, in the Cities of London and Westminster, or within twenty miles thereof, without a Licence had for that Purpose ... shall be deemed a disorderly House or Place ...'.

The Act gave constables the right to enter and seize all persons found therein; the person keeping '... such House, Room, Garden, or other Place' could be fined £100. Licensed premises had to display an inscription 'in some notorious Place over the Door or Entrance' and were not allowed to be open before 'the Hour of Five in the Afternoon'. If either of these conditions were breached, a licence could be revoked.

However the Fourth Clause of this Act declared that 'nothing in this Act contained shall extend or be construed to extend to the Theatres Royal in Drury Lane and Covent Garden, or the Theatre commonly called the King's Theatre in the Haymarket, or any of them, nor to such Performances and public Entertainments as are or shall be lawfully exercised and carried on under or by virtue of Letters Patent, or Licence of the Crown, or the Licence of the Lord Chamberlain of His Majesty's Household ...'.

But perhaps this Act should have been costumed like King George's foot soldiers with headgear that was a cross between a bishop's mitre and a fool's cap. It has ever been thus when Parliament has tried to take the 'band-call'.

Undoubtedly the 1843 Theatres Act was to make the distinction between theatre and music hall, actor and performer, much clearer. Because it made it possible for all places of entertainment holding 'burletta' licences to present stage plays, this broke the monopoly of the Patent Theatres who up to now had been the sole purveyors of legitimate drama; except that where 'any Money or other Reward shall be taken or charged, directly or indirectly, or in which the Purchase of any Article is made a Condition for the Admission of any Person into any Theatre to see any Stage Play, and also in every Case in which any Stage Play shall be acted or presented in any House, Room, or Place in which distilled or fermented Exciseable Liquor shall be sold, every Actor therein shall be deemed to be acting for Hire . . .'. The Act was very specific – the choice meant a 'wet house' and variety or a 'dry house' and drama.

A great many streams joined together to form 'music hall'. The supper rooms and the tavern 'glee clubs' led by Henry Cook's at the Mogul Tavern – now the site of the New London Theatre – brought forward new artistes.

Other streams included the Coal Hole and the Cider Cellar in Fountain Court, The Strand, and in Maiden Lane respectively. Here in 1822, William and John Rhodes presided, and here later, under the regime of Renton Nicholson, notorious for his 'Judge and Jury' shows, W. G. Ross was to sing the awesome *Ballad of Sam Hall*. The contemporary commentators indicate that Ross sang the song with chilling effect and fantastic success for eight years. But he never sustained that success with new songs, and died a 'super' in a Gaiety show.

The birth of music hall is often dated from the opening of the Canterbury by Charles Morton on 17 May 1852.

> . . . Coming to the Canterbury was dreadful. I remember the shock I got when I went under the railway arch, down the dingy, dirty, narrow street, the greasy sidewalk, the muddy gutter, full of dirty babies, the common-place looking public house. I felt I could not go in; but I did. The people were polite, and showed me upstairs; there was lots of sawdust. Soon I found myself in a long picture gallery, at the other end of which a rehearsal was being held . . . the smell of beer and stale tobacco smoke revolted me . . . .

Thus Emily Soldene's memories of auditioning at the Canterbury. But it was at this hall that ladies were permitted to watch the show, and admission was by a sixpenny ticket part of which came back in drinks.

Music hall came and grew out of all the varied means performers used to gain and hold an audience. This was their binding link – their audience. They were the 'loners' of entertainment, jealous of any success they might gain, and well aware that in the words of Marie Lloyd: 'We are here today, and gone tomorrow. You may get a little song tonight and you are a star tomorrow; then you may not get another song, and then what are you going to do?' By a strange irony the Industrial Revolution, which almost destroyed the craftsman's art, was to nurture the music hall with its emphasis on the individual's skills and ingenuity. T. S. Eliot writing in 1923, a year after Marie's death, put it in these words:

The lower class still exists; but perhaps it will not exist for long. In the Music Hall comedians they find the expression and dignity of their own lives; and this is not found in the most elaborate and expensive revue. In England at any rate, the revue expresses almost nothing. . . . The working man who went to the Music Hall and saw Marie Lloyd and joined in the chorus was himself performing part of the act; he was engaged in that collaboration of the audience with the artist which is necessary in all art and most obviously in dramatic art.

MATCHLESS MATCHAM

London, however, had no monopoly in making music hall. In 1868, there were over 300 provincial halls – recognised 'dates' for the growing army of pros. Any student of music hall buildings must have become intrigued by the constant chopping and changing of names that took place in that heyday of the independents before the circuits were all-powerful. And 'Palace', 'Empire' and 'Hippodrome' were stock names; only the towns were different. One notes the 'changes of uses' as music halls become money-spinners even in areas which were otherwise hit by the blight of unemployment. At least three waxworks went 'live' – Mrs Stoll's Parthenon had previously been Bianchi's Waxworks of Liverpool; Springthorpe's in Hull and the Princess Palace at Leeds had both shown in wax.

Flames too have consumed dozens of theatres and music halls over the years. The risks of fire are always present as a glance at any daily newspaper will confirm, and public places need rigorous fire safety regulations. I have played the concertina whilst firemen tramped above putting out a kitchen blaze, and my father was unable to be at my christening because of a cutting-room fire in those nitrate film days. I remember seeing Twickenham Film Studios burn down.

Grandpa's scrapbook includes a spectacular photograph of the destruction of the Pier Pavilion at Cleethorpes in July 1903 together with a racy report by Charlie Coborn who had 'just run down from Grimsby on a tramcar for an airing'. He sent a report to *The Era* in which he described the sight as 'one of the most terribly impressive I ever saw.' There is no doubt that dry weather allied to the usual creosoted wood of the pier's deck would soon overwhelm a pavilion. As Charlie said:

> The tramcar turned into Cleethorpes, and we came in sight of the pier, the flames were projecting from underneath each side of the broad part at the end upon which the pavilion stood, in much the same way as they would show under a kettle upon a gas stove. One of the first people I met was Mr Nelson Hardy, the ventriloquist . . . he had just managed to save his basket containing his figures which he had dragged literally through the flames, and not a moment too soon . . . While I was lamenting the fact that no Cinematograph operator was present to avail himself of such a wonderful opportunity as the whole scene presented, Mr Percy Honri's own Cinematograph was inside, adding food to the flames.

PIER FIRE CLEETHORPES. JULY 6 1903
COPYRIGHT 14089

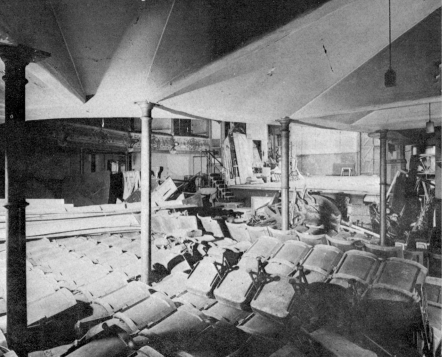

Top, fire at the Pier,
Cleethorpes 1903; right, the
end of the Queen's, Poplar 1959
© G.L.C. Photograph Library

He himself I saw doing yeoman service with the fire-extinguishing apparatus . . . He also had cause to be thankful that, owing to the energetic action of Mr Collinson, the conductor of the Pier orchestra, his very valuable musical instruments had been early removed to a place of safety . . .

Of course, the affair had its humorous aspects . . . Mr Honri declared that he distinctly heard Mr Hardy's figures scream for help . . . Mr Hardy himself earned undying infamy by trotting out that hoary-headed joke about the piano not having been saved because the firemen could not play on it . . . Some of the young men present lamented the loss of the dancing floor and sang together 'Should old acquaintance be forgot' in a singular minor key, as Gilbert puts it. Their lamentations were premature, as Mr Bolland, the manager of the pier, procured and erected a marquee in the grounds the same afternoon, and the entertainment proceeded almost as though nothing had happened . . . .

So here again the old adage rang out – 'The show must go on' and it did, and it does.

Over the years not only blaze and blitz but also the bulldozer exacted the greatest casualties amongst music halls, often under the fashionable pretext of 'rationalisation' or merely 'bookkeeping'. It has taken a long time for people to realise the importance of the theatre as an essential of a civilised community. Maybe we are learning just in time. The closure and the destruction of theatres is an emotive subject, but particularly when one recalls the deliberate destruction not of badly designed and uncomfortable 'flea-pits' but of the music halls designed by Frank Matcham – the matchless Matcham. One thinks of the 'Met' in Edgware Road, Chiswick, Finsbury Park, Leicester, and Chatham, of Ardwick and Walham Green, of the Lyric at Hammersmith, scene of Nigel Playfair's triumphs.

I was on the last bill to work the Palace, Hull, in July 1965, after its sixty-eight years of existence. Percy Honri had been there with *Concordia*, sixty years earlier. Now I was standing in the same place for the last time, linking arms with the rest of the bill and the audience to sing the final *Auld lang syne* for Frank Matcham's Palace of Varieties.

Who was Frank Matcham? There is scant reference to him in the history books of the theatre – the odd footnote or a passing mention that he 'was the most prolific theatre architect of his period; responsible for so many theatres, music halls and opera houses in the late nineteenth century boom, that no precise record can be ascertained . . .'. In a week when Leo Stormont and George Graves were appearing at the London Hippodrome he designed, *Vanity Fair* had chosen him for its regular 'Men of the Day' (5 July 1911).

'. . . Born at Newton Abbot, Devon in 1854.' Other sources quote his date of birth as 1852, the year that Charles Morton opened the Canterbury Music Hall – the first custom-built music hall. A few days after Morton's death Matcham's definitive work, the magnificent Coliseum, opened. So close were the links between

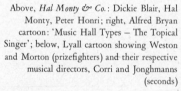

Above, *Hal Monty & Co.*: Dickie Blair, Hal Monty, Peter Honri; right, Alfred Bryan cartoon: 'Music Hall Types – The Topical Singer'; below, Lyall cartoon showing Weston and Morton (prizefighters) and their respective musical directors, Corri and Jonghmanns (seconds)

Gallant Fight for the Championship of the W C District.

the 'father of the halls' and the man who designed the Empires. At the age of fifteen Matcham was articled for a term to a London quantity surveyor, but 'all the while he kept up his architectural drawing by systematic and tireless evening study'. Later he was to join Mr T. Robinson, the Lord Chamberlain's architect, and marry his youngest daughter. 'Theatrical design seemed to possess for him a peculiar fascination . . . he boldly adventured into practice for himself, and was enabled to follow, on his own lines, the branch of the profession he now so conspicuously adorns. . . .' Frank Matcham lived until 1920, and his designs have stood the test of time – there was no need for Matcham theatres to be trendy; they were built to enable an enthusiastic theatre or music hall audience to see and hear everything in comfort. Whether he was designing to the budget laid down by Oswald Stoll for the Coliseum in St Martin's Lane, to Dan Leno and Harry Randall's Granville at Walham Green or the Opera House Cheltenham, Matcham achieved a perfect balance between the audience and the entertainers. At the age of thirty-one, he had designed the new Grand Theatre, Islington, for Morton. Rising like a phoenix out of the ashes of the Philharmonic Theatre burnt down in 1882, the first Grand Theatre, opened in 1883, had only four years of life before it too was consumed by flames. Morton entrusted the design to Matcham again and the second Grand opened in 1888, surviving for twelve years – after which it burned down yet again! Although it was replaced, Frank Matcham had by then designed many other leading music halls and theatres – including the Tivoli (1890), Paragon (1893), 'Met' (1897), Richmond (1899) and London Hippodrome (1900).

In his autobiography *Harry Randall – Old Time Comedian*, Harry wrote about his music hall builder partnership with Dan Leno and Herbert Campbell:

> . . . Leno, Campbell and myself conceived the idea of going into music hall management. Fred Williams joined us, and our first enterprise was the taking over of a place called Muntz Hall, just by Clapham Junction. . . . We renamed the place 'The Grand Hall, Clapham'. It was a small hall holding about six or seven hundred people. We gave it a great send off by the entire Board appearing the first week. I may remark, however, that we didn't draw our usual salaries! . . . We leased a hall at Croydon and renamed it the 'Empire', it belonged to a man known as 'Spangle' Hales. . . . We bought a piece of ground at Walham Green, formed a company and built the 'Granville'. Our architect who took a friendly interest in us, was the celebrated theatre designer Frank Matcham . . . . The interior of this little theatre was entirely decorated with faience-work carried out by Doultons. It was the first to be decorated in this way, which possessed a double advantage; it was easily washed down and always looked fresh.

Built in 1897/8, the Granville had indeed anticipated the concept that plaster cupids and gargoyles were unhygienic. But Matcham's introduction of the 'Eburite faience tiles' was not dogmatic. His Richmond Theatre opened on 18 September

1899 and had auditorium decorations 'which are in the Elizabethan style, are rich, and yet characterised by an artistic reserve which is most pleasing to the eye. The gilt moulding set off by crimson hangings and upholstery, form a welcome combination of light and warmth.'

During the next decade Matcham ensured not only that London had a high output of new luxury music halls – 'palaces of varieties' – but that most provincial cities also bore the Matcham hallmark.

Matcham's magic was to give a 3,000 seater the intimacy of a theatre one third of that capacity. Not only could he build to a budget, he designed highly individual theatres and he worked fast. The 'Met' was built for Henri Gros in four months after the foundation stone was laid on 17 August 1897. Oswald Stoll opened his New Middlesex Music Hall a mere week ahead of Alfred Butt's Victoria Palace, built on the site of the Standard, Pimlico, the first London hall where the Thompson Trio had worked.

Three theatres out of the hundred or more Matcham designed place him in a class of his own: the Hippodrome (1900), the Coliseum (1904) and the Palladium (1910). Thankfully these theatres are still with us, only the Hippodrome having undergone major interior alterations to become the 'Talk of the Town'. When Stoll commissioned Matcham to design his Coliseum, he wanted it to exceed Drury Lane in size, and he was willing to pay an extra £70,000 for the unique 'three concentric circles' revolving stage capable of moving in either direction. Matcham and Stoll visited the United States to examine the new developments in theatre design there, and it is a tribute to him that for fifty years almost no changes were made in the design of the Coliseum.

Astonishingly, the Palladium was originally to have been called the Arena, with a capacity of 5,000. Gibbons's LTV circuit bought Hengler's Cirque in 1908 as a site for the biggest 'palace of varieties'. On the advice of Matcham, Walter Gibbons agreed that it would be impossible to get the intimate music hall atmosphere with 5,000 seats. So the present Palladium was born, and is still the heart of music hall and variety. Matcham designed other theatres before he died, but none to surpass the Palladium – his definitive work. Who can fail to echo the words of the reporter who wrote, in his opening night review: '. . . the magnificent sweep of the dress circle presents a remarkable appearance from the stage.'

'. . . WHO SANG A MOST TOPICAL SONG . . .'

It seems funny to find in a book published in 1908 a reference to 'old music hall songs'; but music hall had been firmly established for over sixty years in the same recognisable form, and whilst fashions changed more slowly in those days – they did change. Referring to the songs of the period between the early sixties and the late eighties of the last century, Ralph Nevill says, in *Piccadilly to Pall Mall*, written in collaboration with Charles Edward Jerningham:

> In those days every important incident or event gave birth to a popular comic
> song. 'Angelina was always fond of Soldiers' commemorated the visit of

the Belgian Volunteers to London in 1868. 'Champagne Charlie', 'Moet & Chandon' and 'Clicquot' marked the commencement of the popularity of champagne in this country. 'The Galloping Snob' perpetuated the overthrow of Sir Richard Mayne — then Commissioner of Police — in Hyde Park in 1867. 'Immensikoff' marked the introduction of fur coats, and 'Would you be surprised to hear!' was founded on the phrase continually used by Sir John Coleridge . . . when cross-examining the Tichborne Claimant in 1872. . . .

In the early eighties Nellie Farren and Alfred Vance ridiculed the youth of the day who wore blue trousers, black coats and white neckties, carried a crutch with their elbows out at right angles, and had a toothpick always between the teeth. Part of the chorus of one particular song about the 'toothpick and crutch brigade' goes:

> How do you like London, how do you like Town?
> How do you like the Strand, dear,
>   now Temple Bar's pulled down?
> How do you like the lardi-da, the toothpick and the crutch?
> How did you get those trousers on,
>   and did they hurt you much? . . .

But the 'lardi-da' send-up would as often be followed by a realistic song of hard times — times audiences knew were with them, just around the corner. Here is Florrie Gallimore singing the more deeply evocative:

> It's the poor wot 'elps the poor
> When poverty knocks at the door,
> Those wot live in mansions grand
> Orften fail to understand
> The meanin' of that little word
> 'Unger, I am shore
> But the poor they know
> The meanin' and so
> It's the poor wot 'elps the poor. . .

Just as the halls would comment on social conditions, so they could be forthright on social customs and behaviour. Prudes have never been able to accept the view of the critic James Agate: '. . . the great virtue of the music hall is that it jokes openly of those things which are commonly discussed in bar parlours.' In 1970, John Huntley wrote to *The Call Boy* — the journal of the British Music Hall Society — that having 'always been extremely proud of the fact that Music Hall was the original "permissive society" and went such a long way to recognising the utter stupidity of the artificially refined exterior with which Victorian society attempted to cover up its less savoury truths, I remain staggered at the endless attempts now being made to pretend that things were otherwise . . .'. Whilst house contracts engaging artistes bristled with 'instant dismissal' clauses for 'giving

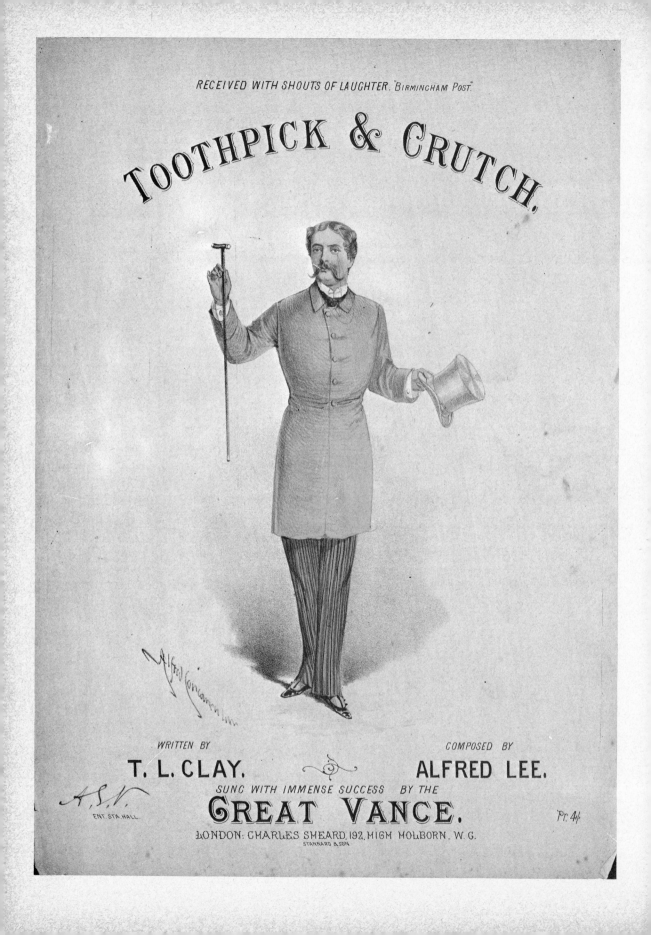

expression to any vulgarity or words having a double meaning' – a 1905 day bill of the Royal Cambridge, Bishopsgate, starred Frederick Maxwell's Company supported by 'the Talented Actress Miss Lois Du Cane, in the Sensational Domestic Episode "The Girl I love",' and ending with the advice in capital letters: 'SEE THE SENSATIONAL FLOGGING SCENE'. One wonders if Miss Du Cane was involved in that scene! John Huntley went on to recall Arnold Bennett's comment in his *Journals*, published in 1910, on seeing Marie Lloyd's turn at the Tivoli on 31 December 1909:

> Sunday: Jan 2nd 1910. On Friday night, out last night in London, we went to the Tivoli. There were no seats except in the pit, so we went in the pit. Little Tich was very good and George Formby, the Lancashire comedian, was perhaps even better. Gus Elen I did not care for. And I couldn't see the legendary cleverness of the vulgarity of Marie Lloyd. She was very young and spry for a grandmother. All her songs were variations on the same theme of sexual naughtiness. No censor would ever pass them, and especially he wouldn't pass her winks and silences.

I share John Huntley's view that Marie was one of the first people to recognise a principle of modern society that there was a great deal to be said for 'doing and speaking in public what Victorian society did in private'. It's not so long ago that Max Miller would admonish his audience: 'It's people like you that get me a bad name!' The performer constantly juggles with words – there may be a hundred nuances that can be put in a phrase, and the top pro must be able to select instantly the right one every time. This is where experience and constant practice pay off. When I worked with Hal Monty as a 'feed' for nearly two years, he often practised tongue-twisters – and had a routine about 'a shooting brake shooting up Shooters Hill'. Hal Monty's forte was as a 'stand up comedian' – and his 'Letter' was quite a classic:

> Dear Son – This is your Mum writing to you. It's hotter now than it was, and it's not so hot as what it is – ain't it?

His staccato delivery, and the cocky manner were as much a product of the post-war rationing era, the golden age of the barrow boy, as the 'heavy swell' has become identified with the 1860s.

A PRIDE OF LION COMIQUES

As music hall expanded, so came the personalities who identified themselves with a 'character' and often with an individual hall, the Oxford, Weston's or the London Pavilion. The Pav's programme in the seventies used to be the current edition of *The Entr'acte* with the names of the performers – who would be announced with due ceremony by Harry Cavendish, 'The Chair' – facing one of Alfred Bryan's cartoons. It cost one penny, whilst seats at marble tables at the sides of the stage cost sixpence, and for half-a-crown you sat with 'Mr Chairman'. The beer was twopence a glass. There were eighteen or twenty turns, the show starting at 7.30

Alfred Concanen song cover of the Great Vance

and ending at midnight. And this was where comic singers like George Leybourne, Arthur Lloyd, G. H. Macdermott, Alfred Vance, Harry Rickards and Jolly John Nash came to the fore.

The author M. Willson Disher tells us:

> . . . the heavy swell who went on the spree was not invented until a mechanic from the Midlands came to London for work, sang in the East End as Joe Saunders, and was set by Charles Morton before the worshipping eyes of the Canterbury as George Leybourne or Champagne Charlie. On the stage he was as gilded as Lord Dundreary . . . . In 'Champagne Charlie' he voiced sentiments so agreeable to rebels against Victorian respectability that his salary went up to £120 a week . . . . Every day was a holiday; his pockets filled as soon as they emptied.

In my music hall documentary about working 'turns', *10.20 The Oxford, Doubling the Paragon*, I introduce Ferdy Jongmanns, musical director at the Canterbury, who announces three of those 'heavy swells' or 'lion comiques' as they came to be known:

> 'The guvnor, Mr Morton, has always been fond of the lardi-da y'know; and so was his rival Ted Weston, proprietor of the Royal Holborn. In fact, there was a cartoon of the two of 'em prizefighting for the 'Championship of the West Central District' with myself as Mr Morton's second and little Corri, Mr Weston's M.D. as his.'

The era of what Mr Poole called the lion comiques had arrived; and sponsored by the rival music hall proprietors they vied for the public's adulation. With their dandy ways, their toppers and whiskers, and their constant reference to 'fizz', they were the Showmen of the Halls: G. H. Macdermott at the London Pavilion, George Leybourne at the Royal Holborn and Alfred Vance – the Great Vance, they called him – at the Oxford.

'Ladies and Gentlemen, Mr George Leybourne – "Champagne Charlie" – with his new song dedicated to Monsewer Leotard – "The Man on the Flying Trapeze".'

My second lion comique, G. H. Macdermott, was associated with far more than *The Jingo Song*; his comedy material would cover all the hundred and one themes of the comic singer – mothers-in-law, kippers and all.

In one of my scenes, we find Gilbert Hastings Macdermott at home wearing an elegant quilted smoking jacket. His rooms are well furnished, and sepia photographs of Disraeli and the Prince of Wales are prominently displayed. He pours himself a stiff brandy, and lights a cheroot. A bell rings off stage, and a murmur of voices is heard. There is a discreet knock on the door, and his valet Wilkins enters:

'Excuse me sir, Mr Hunt has called and wishes to speak with you.'

'Does he, Wilkins?'

H. R. JACOBS'
Clark Street Theatre,
H. R. JACOBS, Sole Manager.

MATINEES SUNDAY, THURSDAY AND SATURDAY.
Best Seats at any Matinee, 25c and 50c.

Commencing Sunday Matinee, May 14th, 1893,

And continuing until further notice,

Tony Pastor's Company
—— OF ——

American and European Vaudeville Novelties.

The Comic Acrobats,
THE SCHALLERS,
The Famous Knockabouts.

THE TWO EMERALDS,
EILEEN and NORA O'SHEA,
Irish Song and Dance Artists.

TONY PASTOR'S TIMELY TOPICS.

THE NAWNS,
In thsir Comedy Creation WRINKLETS.

MISS PAM LE BLANCHE,
English Dancing Soubrette.

THE THOMPSON TRIO,
Artistic and Comic Musical Trio, Presenting an Act new to America.
Original, Comical, Artistic and Delightful.

WARD AND VOKES,
As HAROLD and PERCY, from Harvard.

Top left, passenger list 1893 for Thompson Trio's voyage to America; top right, the Trio's appearance on Tony Pastor's *Chicago Fair* bill; cartoon envelope to Percy Honri on his solo tour of U.S.A. 1899

'He is most anxious to see you at once, sir.'

'Then, my dear fellow, we must accommodate him. I feared it might be some dunner – remember Wilkins, always to refer them to Mr Edwin Villiers care of the "Pav". Show Mr Hunt in, Wilkins.'

'Very well, sir' and the valet glides out of the room noiselessly.

The ornate clock on the mantlepiece strikes the quarter, as Wilkins knocks and introduces the songwriter G. W. Hunt. 'Jingo' Hunt is florid in face and in manner. Macdermott begins to pour another brandy for his surprise guest.

'Good day to you, Macdermott – er – thanks, I have got a bit of a chest today. Well, have you read the papers?'

Macdermott shakes his head. 'Is Leybourne dead? Has he fallen off his trapeze into a magnum of fizz?'

Hunt almost splutters out his news: 'No, Gilbert. It's Charles Dilke . . .'

'Gladstone's bright young man? – been run over by a Tory cabbie!'

With an air of triumph, Hunt exclaims: 'Better than that, laddie – friend Dilke has been less than discreet with his favours . . .'

'Trust "True Blue" Hunt to hear about that – has he been visiting that little place you have in Peckham Rye?'

Hunt smiles sheepishly: 'If I didn't know you better, I'd consider that an insult to me, and to a good lady's honour.'

'Come, Hunt, spill the milk of human kindness . . .'

'Jingo' Hunt rises sharply: 'Laddie, what did you say . . . spill the milk?'

Macdermott nods, and grins as Hunt pulls out an old envelope and starts scribbling furiously:

'How's this sound – eh? Charles Dilke spilt the milk taking it home to Chelsea. The papers say that Charlie's gay, rather a wilful wag. This noble representative of everything good in Chelsea has let the cat, the naughty cat, right out of the Gladstone bag.'

Macdermott has put aside his cheroot, and leans towards Hunt: 'So now you're writing for the old "Thunderer"'.

Hunt starts to hum a tune, but breaks off, and points a stubby finger at Macdermott: 'No, it's for your turn tonight at the "Pav" – the papers will be full of it tonight . . . the time is ripe. Where's your banjo? Here's the tune.'

Macdermott picks up his banjo from behind his chair, and as Hunt hums the melody, begins to pick out some chords:

'Hunt, you're on for a dozen bottles of brandy – the Liberals will love me for this song . . . "Charles Dilke spilt the milk . . .".'

Alfred Vance, was born Alfred Peck Stevens. A full page in *The Era Almanack Advertiser* for 1872 describes him as 'Author, Composer, Buffo Vocalist, and Comedian . . .' and thirty 'write-ups' from all over the country are concluded by this review from *The Oxford Undergrad's Journal*, 2 November 1871:

> . . . Vance's humour gave us the impression of coming very near to Sydney
> Smith's definition of true wit. Vance is not a mere portrayer of other people's

compositions, but he portrays his own; and, as the real founder of the modern school of refined comic singing, and as its master, par excellence, Vance receives the support of Oxford, for he admires the genuine article, and has no favours for the host of imitators which has lately sprung up like a bed of mushrooms . . . .

Vance enjoyed the friendship of the Prince of Wales, and was known as the 'Beau Brummel of the Halls'.

Recreating Great Vance in my play I have him entering with a flourish. Soon you and a packed 'Pav' are joining in:

> Slap Bang, Here we are again!
> Here we are again! Here we are again!
> Slap Bang, Here are are again
> Rare merry dogs are we! — *Blackout*

The lights come up to reveal George Leybourne pouring champagne into a glass as Vance re-enters: 'My dear Alfred, will you join me in some fizz? I hear Morton only gives you water, what? There's plenty more where this comes from . . . my brougham is always well corked when I "champagne". . . .'

Vance adjusts his lavender-coloured gloves, and smooths the ribbon on his silk hat: 'My thanks, George — I'd heard that Weston had been stabling your four nags in the pit at the Royal Holborn — and there was room to spare?'

'So the chickaleary bloke has forgotten his coster character. There are crowds in to hear "Champagne Charlie",' Leybourne replies with a laugh.

'True, of course, George — but only because they couldn't get in to see me!'

Suddenly Leybourne exclaims: 'Hide the fizz — here's Macdermott.'

Macdermott enters carrying a binder full of manuscript music under his arm: 'Ah ha — the two Obadiahs. — One's higher than the other. Hush — here comes the bogey man.'

Alfred Vance exchanges a look with Leybourne: 'Macdermott! — that must have taken you an age to work out. Leybourne and I were discussing higher things — the opening of the Suez Canal, Jolly Nash's Presidency of the Music Hall Sickness Fund and Provident Society, and a wager on the house each plays to tomorrow night.'

Quite unruffled, Macdermott opens the music binder: 'I get crowds round the stage door — yes crowds daring me to come out!' He starts to hand out some manuscript bearing lyrics in a copper-plate hand: 'But let's try this new song Hunt wrote for me — got a good tune too. But Jingo's asking a fiver for it — trust him to ask that much for a song that might last a week. "Dear old pals" he calls it, the only thing dear about it is the cost.'

They all begin to sing:

> Dear old pals, jolly old pals,
> Clinging together in all sorts of weather . . .

Percy Honri has just played our Circuit and has made a
favorable impression. His specialty, consisting of Concertina
and Vocal solos is really very clever and of a refined order,
a fitting number for any bill.

Yours Truly

John Morrisey
Manager
Orpheum Theatre
S.F. Cal

San Francisco theatre manager's
reference; stills by De Youngs of
Broadway 1899

. . . A glimpse at the colourful 'lion comiques', whose showmanship and aplomb is carried on today by artistes like Liberace and Danny La Rue.

THE 'PASTORISED' VARIETY

On March 8th 1893 the White Star steamship *Majestic* left Liverpool for New York. On board was the Thompson Trio bound for their American debut at the famous Tony Pastor's theatre in Fourteenth Street. With the Emerald Sisters, Miss Pam Le Blanche and the Schallers, the Thompson Trio assisted at an entertainment on board given in aid of the Seaman's Orphanage, which netted that benevolent institution £36 . . . This is what the famed *New York Clipper* had to say about their first performance in the New World:

> Eileen and Nora O'Shea, styled the Two Emeralds made their American debut on Monday night March 20th. They are singers and dancers of a good sort, and won flattering recognition. The Thompson Trio also made their first appearance in America. The Trio are exceptionally clever musicians, playing on oddly shaped instruments with much skill and in pleasing harmony . . .

Tony Pastor's New Fourteenth Street Theatre had a capacity of a few hundred — 'a bandbox hewn out of Tammany Hall, which then adjoined the Academy of Music at the corner of Irving Place, it was not new nor much of a theater', was how Douglas Gilbert described it in his monumental book *American vaudeville — its life and times*. But here in 1881, vaudeville had been born; Pastor had learned to double his potential audience by giving shows that offered 'unblushing entertainment' — and was therefore acceptable as a purveyor of entertainment to the wives, sisters and sweethearts. By 1893, he was about the only person to give an out and out variety entertainment. As a contemporary put it: 'Everything is from the French music halls now, all the variety entertainments are given up to the skirt dancer and the eccentric dancers from Paris and their imitators in this country. There is nothing of this kind on Tony Pastor's program. It is vaudeville of the English not of the naughty French sort.'

The Thompson Trio's American tour read: Weeks 20 & 27 March: Pastor's New York; 3 April: Howard Athenaeum Boston; 10 April: Hyde & Behman's Brooklyn N.Y.; 17 April: Gayety Williamsburgh N.Y.; 24 April: Columbus Harlem N.Y.; 1 May: Whitneys Opera Detroit; 8 & 15 May: Clark Street Chicago; 22 May: Shea & Eberhart's Buffalo; 29 May, 5 & 12 June: Pastor's New York; 19 June, 26 June and 3 July: Imperial Broadway; 10 July: Shea & Eberhart's Buffalo. On 31 July, they were touring Scotland again with Willie (W.F.) Frame. But 1893 had also been Chicago's World Fair year, and Percy had demonstrated his Laechenal concertina on their stand at the Fair. Amy Leslie's column in *The Daily News* of 9 May captures the frolicsome America of the Nineties:

> . . . Tony Pastor's congress of fascination is over at the Clark street theater,

and though a long way off from the boulevards and Midway plaisance is still near enough a more reliable civilization than haunts the Jackson park magnets. The theater was packed as Tony's own in New York would scarcely hope to be this time of the year. Like all of Jacobs' theaters it is pretty, enlivening and manned with an army of polite ushers. Ladies stylish and handsome, crowds of contented young men and sedate families occupied the choicest seats. There was an air of familiarity about the gathering, as if either the audience was made up of visitors who, equally strange in town, felt a bond of union in this alien friendliness or who were accustomed frequenters of this comfortable north side place of amusement. . . . I hied me there for complete forgetfulness of things more tragic. During the day I had swallowed mentally considerable of Phoebe Couzius, quorums, agitations, Columbia brass bands, broken telephones, crossed telegraph wires and World's-Fair red-tape, so felt in a mood bordering upon poetry or suicide. To avoid either I made a bee-line for the Clark street theater and live to tell how much the show delighted.

Tony has a very good show. The Russells are always stars in any variety entertainment . . . the Russell boys captured the comedy palm . . . Pam Le Blanche is cunning and a good dancer. She sings in the trying English music-hall fashion, but is rather a chic little actress. She is dark and eerie, with clouds of gipsy hair about her small face, and, dressed in scarlet, she looked like an unruly flame of motion. Two bright Irish girls Eileen and Nora O'Shea dance and do some entertaining singing, with lightning changes not startling in the hurry but effective in make-up. Bonnie Thornton is dainty . . . and easily recognised as an American woman, but she is unconscionably slow and colorless.

The woman who completely takes the audience by storm is Lizzie Raymond, a daring young creature with a wealth of smiles and saucy airs. . . . Her assaults upon Terpsichore are reckless and unlimited, principally muscular and astonishingly vague, but fascinating to the gallery and exciting to those less forewarned of probabilities . . . and the Thompsons have one of those variable, indispensable and definitely heinous perpetrations of music upon instruments not recommended or insisted upon by vendor Thomas of the World's Fair. There is something fearful in those comic distortions of sounds from fans, flannel dogs, tin steam cars and plaid neckties. Nothing in a wardrobe or kitchen menage is free from the onslaught of these trick musicians. Thompson pere is a decidedly funny comedian. (I make the distinction because variety comedians are dubiously saddening at times.) Young Percy has a gentle musical face, plays beautifully on the harmonicon and sings very sweetly. The entire act was received with cheers of satisfaction from the audience. Ward and Vokes have a great sketch which they handle with fair appreciation . . . any old 'Hasty Pudding' boys of Harvard in town would hurrah at the racy parody on the howling college-swell. Last but not least,

Tony the immortal; bulwark of the buck-dance and double-shuffle! Pedestal of the wily motto-song and chameleon topical gag! . . . To be sure, as preluding remarks suggest, the Clark Street theater is some distance from the Mecca of all songsters' divinest hopes just now, but Tony's place is right in the celebration, top seat, first bandwagon. . . . He has a place in the history of the country and the stage. Mr Pastor can have the front page of my album of celebrities any day he requests it.

Whilst they were in America, Harry took a great fancy to tobacco that included molasses in the mixture. He decided to take a quantity back to England inside the harmonium used in the act. Upon disembarking they passed through customs; no one asked them to play the harmonium but then a molasses base tobacco inside a confined space in July leaves some after-effects. For months Grandpa was nearly asphyxiated by the odour of molasses when he played the harmonium!

KEITH & ORPHEUM CIRCUIT

Crisp one line 'write-offs', a brittle slickness or alternatively a pseudo-cloying turn of phrase seems to be an essential ingredient for the American critic, and when Grandpa returned to New York as a single act in 1898, his 'cuttings' seem to bear this out. *The Sun* reviewed his debut at Keith's Union Square Theatre New York on November 16th as: '. . . A musician as ecstatic as Von Biene is in the roster at Keith's . . . they demand an encore and he responds with a "mother song". He plays his instrument and sings with so much feeling that the gold braid on more than half of the seventeen Keith head ushers may be expected to melt. He is the real thing in tenderness.'

I can imagine Grandpa puzzling over a formula for his act's tour of the Keith and Orpheum circuits. The *Cincinatti Post* might like the way he 'introduces his act with a neat little speech about music, and is unusually clever . . .'; yet in the *Los Angeles Herald's* eyes 'the ladylike Mr Percy Honri is really an artist in his way – when he does not sing'. The *Herald's* rival *The Times* would have to differ and state that 'he discloses a speaking and singing voice that is quite as melodious as his little octagonal music box'. Whilst at Philadelphia *The Item* trotted out their expertise on concertinas and their players with the phrase: '. . . showed a few twists on the concertina that were made known by neither Dutch Daly nor Joe Cawthorn . . .'.

In the late nineties the New York *Morning Telegraph* carried a regular column by Chicot. This was the pseudonym of Epes W. Sargent who later with Sime Silverman founded the Broadway weekly *Variety*. Douglas Gilbert dubs him the first critical commentator of vaudeville:

Chicot's influence on the development of vaudeville can hardly be overestimated. Managers and public accepted his analyses first sceptically, then with enthusiasm. Both were grateful for guidance, and lazy or indifferent performers, realizing that bad notices might lead to cancellation, sought to

Above, Peter Honri in *Ace of Spades* with Ernest Palmer and
George Pearson 1934

Peter Honri in BFI's *Laughing Gas* 1968

better their routines. . . . Chicot was a born crusader, years ahead of his time. He raged at the hokum and bathos that enraptured the sentimental nineties, and his honest opinions . . . were influenced only by merit. . . . His disregard of big names is astonishing. He considered Vesta Tilley, an English music hall artist of considerable draw, an ordinary entertainer and so wrote. . . .

It is nice to know that Grandpa didn't get a Chicot 'caustique':

Percy Honri is a newcomer who understands playing the concertina, and though he spoiled things at the finish by trying to sing, he gave us an overture played in a really creditable fashion. He uses big boxes and makes noise enough for a whole band, but he plays with restraint and a nicer appreciation of values than might be expected. He has a rather mincing manner, which does not prepossess but that can be toned down . . . .

Vaudeville days of Tony Pastor's era have been a favourite stamping ground of the Hollywood musical, the genre that is constantly revived on the television without paying a penny to the actors and actresses that made them. Do you remember the goddesses of those musicals of the forties and fifties – Hayworth, Lamour, Garland and Grable? For a few short weeks in 1969 at the Glasgow Alhambra and at the Palace Theatre in London I worked with one of those goddesses – Betty Grable. It was a happy show thanks to Betty, and I can never forget the ovation that greeted her first entrance as 'Belle Starr' – miscast she may have been as the 'madame' of an 1881 bordello in what was Fort Baker and is now known as Las Vegas but still the multi-million dollar personality shone through. This 'Wild West' musical had some of the corniest dialogue imaginable – the sort of dialogue and hokum that would make the Crazy Gang seem positively sophisticated.

THAT NEW NOVELTY – THE BIOSCOPE

'Laughing Gas. Britain 1968. A popular comic song that was originally performed in the music halls of the 1830s. Transcribed for concertina accompaniment it is here performed at the Leeds City Varieties Theatre by Peter Honri. Running time 4 minutes' – this is how the British Film Institute catalogue of music hall films describes a film that was originally made for the 1968 World Congress of Anaesthetists.

Dr Denis Smith, an authority on anaesthetics, had thought of reconstructing the song on film as an illustration for the paper he was presenting at the Congress, and had arranged with the British Film Institute to film it. I was approached to sing the song about Jeremy Jones, a professional mourner who swallows a bladder of 'laughing gas'. Dr Smith arranged for us to film the song at the famous City Varieties, and with the help of Albert Pegg everything was prepared for Bruce Beresford of the B.F.I. to make the short film to a scenario that I had written.

The inclusion of this song in a learned lecture was not frivolous, but played a part in the story of the start of anaesthetics as an aid to medicine. It seems that whilst Humphry Davy was experimenting with nitrous oxide at the end of the eighteenth century, he happened to be suffering from toothache – he inhaled some of the gas and found not only that it was exhilarating, but that the toothache vanished. The pleasurable sensations of 'laughing gas' caught the public fancy:

> . . . Poor Jeremy Jones, long sought for relief
> For of Mourners, he really was the Chief;
> His nerves were shook — he was thin as a leaf
> And his flesh was worn from his bones with grief.
> Ha ha ho ho he he too ral ral loo ral loo.
>
> A Wag, who heard of poor Jeremy's case,
> Told him, He'd very soon alter his face,
> Invited him home and while there, alas!
> He swallowed a bladder of Laughing Gas!
> Ha ha ho ho he he too ral ral loo ral loo.
>
> As soon as Poor Jeremy swallowed the dose,
> A horrible peal of laughter arose,
> He paid no attention, to friends, or to foes,
> As convulsed with laughter, he homeward goes,
> Ha ha ho ho he he too ral ral loo ral loo . . . .

Laughing gas was not my first solo on film. Thirty-four years earlier I had piped 'Vote for Trent — don't put it in 'is eye, put it in 'is mouth', and with these memorable words I had become a few feet of sprocket holes in one of the many 'quota quickies' made by Twickenham Film Studios in 1934. The film was *Ace of Spades* and starred Dickie Cooper as a breathless, bumbling young parliamentary candidate. I was one of those four year old scene-stealers, and I had to heckle the luckless candidate whilst he minded the baby for Mum who had gone to vote for his rival 'Trent'. Uncle Dickie was not at all proficient with the baby's bottle!

These pictures were 'shot' in a fortnight, and although I didn't realise it, my director was George Pearson, the doyen of British film directors at that time. The cameraman was Ernest Palmer, and my words were recorded on the Visatone Sound System by my father Baynham Honri. At the end of the day, my Post Office Savings Book had increased by one pound, and I had a shilling for myself and a still from 'Uncle Cyril' — Cyril Stanborough.

My father recalls his first meeting with George Pearson in an article for *The Silent Picture*:

> . . . The year was 1913. Or was it 1914? Anyway, the place was the Alexandra Palace. And it was through a crack in the door of the former 'learners' ice skating rink that a boy aged nine had a first glimpse of a film studio. Through that crack came the violet light of arc lamps illuminating a piece of scenery at the end of a room and a Pathe film camera in the foreground. Next to the camera, two moustached gentlemen in bowler hats discussed a problem. They were George Pearson (producer) and L. C. Macbean (studio manager). The boy looking through the door crack was me. What I

Bohemia: Percy Honri's
'Mephisto' and 'Sheik'; Percy
with his Silver Band 1911

saw was the studio of the Union Film Publishing Co. Ltd – trade mark: Big Ben. This was a subsidiary of Pathe Freres Cinema Ltd ... the film was called *Heroes of the Mine*. ... That was when I first decided to be a 'film manufacturer', which was the fiscal name given to film producers then .... Later when the talkies arrived, and I recorded several films for him, he did not throw his hat on the floor and jump on it, when the microphones inevitably crackled or a railway train rumbled past the studios. ...

George Pearson himself remembers those early days. In *Flashback – the Autobiography of a British Film Maker* George Pearson, O.B.E., wrote:

... inside the Palace there was a theatre, and a young lad in some way connected with its staff, often watched me at work on the outdoor stage; that lad, Baynham Honri, became in manhood a famous film technician, eventually elected as President of the British Kinematograph Society, the premier scientific association of British filmdom. In later years we renewed that early friendship and have maintained it ever since ....

George Pearson died in February 1973 – his friendship with my father had lasted sixty years.

My father had been at Alexandra Palace because Percy Honri had established rehearsal rooms and a scene dock there for *Bohemia* – the successor to *Concordia*, and the wartime *Quick March* show which he publicised in a *Daily Mail* front page cartoon as 'Percy Honri's 1915 Revue' – a daring fashion in those days. Percy's association with the 'Ally Pally' had begun when he decided to produce an al fresco pierrot show there for the 1909 season, managed by my great-grandfather Harry Tomps. The *News of the World* said:

... Under the shade of some magnificent old trees on the breeze-swept heights of the Alexandra Palace ... Percy Honri has established an al fresco entertainment which opened yesterday, and will be given three times daily throughout the season. In the hot weather when the music halls are like Turkish baths, the amusement seeker will find nothing more pleasant than a couple of hours with Percy Honri's Pierrots, a clever band of entertainers, whose repertoires are quite up-to-date .... The Pierrots should be the popular resort of North Londoners, especially as the trams take one direct to the hall under the sky. ...

The Era commented that 'apart from the merit of the performance, the fine electric lightning at the evening show is a feature worthy of mention...'. The *Encore*, however, thought they were a little too serious for Pierrots, and said: 'Now then, Percy, just wake them up, and put some mirth and merriment into the programme.'

Later on, Grandpa introduced band concerts here with his own silver band which became a feature of the later editions of *Concordia* and his later revues. Many years later at a 'Water Rat' function, Jack Hylton said that it was seeing Percy Honri's band at one of the Broadhead halls that made him determined to have his

A photograph with a succession of pictures forming a Cinematograph film representing "a Moon" which rises from behind a hill, & which makes grimaces & the face being that photographed from a human being. At a given time there appears a little body under the moon's face together with a banjo which the figure is supposed to play but eventually breaks out with a look of disgust the figure complete picture sinks down behind the hill.

I do hereby give Mr.
Percy Honri, permission
to sing "Oh Mr. Moon" on the
Music Halls
B. Feldman

Top, probably the earliest British film scenario — for Mitchell and Kenyon's film of Percy Honri as 'Mr Moon' — 1901; far left, Bert Feldman's assignment of the song *Oh Mr Moon* 1901; bottom left, frames from the original film; left, *Era* proof of the new act with its 'cinematograph novelty'

PERCY
HONRI IN CONCORDIA

PERCY HONRI
AT THE OXFORD.

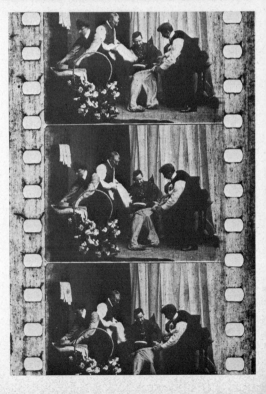

Concordia: top left, poster; above left, cartoon from
The News of the World; above right, stage photo showing screen
on which 'Mr Moon' was projected; right, frames from
Charles Urban's the 'Quick Change Dressing Room' 1908

own 'Big Band on Stage' at a music hall. Before 'big bands' became the almost permanent fixture of music hall bills in the 1930s, the bioscope had entered as an 'extra turn'.

The first public showing of motion pictures on a screen in London took place at the Regent Street Polytechnic in 1895, as part of a magic show by 'Professor' Trewey, a French illusionist. He had been filmed doing conjuring tricks and manipulating a flexible hat to resemble Wellington, Nelson and Napoleon. A few weeks later Robert Paul converted an Edison Kinetoscope – a single viewer peep-hole machine – so that the films could be projected on to a screen at the Alhambra Music Hall in Leicester Square as an 'end turn'. In *Milestones in Motion Picture Production*, my father Baynham describes Robert Paul as being at that time '... the most advanced British animated picture man in England, whose "Theatrograph" projector had its name changed to "Animatograph" due to a mistake in a Court Circular. This Court Circular referred to an "Animatograph display before the Prince of Wales", a mistake made by Prince Edward himself after seeing the film of his horse winning the Derby. Paul immediately changed the name of his apparatus to Animatograph "by Royal request". Quite a showman was this brilliant engineer. . . .' The popularity of the Alhambra's 'animatograph' ensured that other West End music halls followed suit – the Pavilion, Tivoli, Palace and Oxford were all soon showing films as an extra turn – topicals in most cases, the forerunners of newsreels. They were 500 feet in length, and ran for approximately eight minutes at sixteen frames a second – roughly the speed the operators turned the handles!

I suppose our involvement with films really began in 1901 when Percy was working Frank MacNaghten's Palace Theatre at Blackburn. On the bill with him were not the usual scratchy 'topicals', but living pictures made by two local film manufacturers, S. Mitchell and James Kenyon. Kenyon was in business with his father as a house furnisher in King Street, Blackburn, and used a back garden studio platform, relying solely on sunlight to get an exposure. Many of the 'Boer War topicals' were actually filmed on the nearby Yellow Hills. One of the songs in Grandpa's act that week was *Oh, Mr Moon*, composed by Frederick Norton and recently published by Bert Feldman. Percy had the idea he could utilise the bioscope in his act, projecting 'Mr Moon' on to the backcloth suitably painted, and singing the song to the flickering image; and so he wrote this scenario:

> A photograph with a succession of pictures forming a Cinematograph film representing 'A Moon' which rises from behind a hill and makes grimaces – the face being photographed from a human being. At a given time there appears a little body under the moon's face together with a banjo which the figure is supposed to play but eventually breaks and with a look of disgust the complete picture sinks down behind the hill.

Possibly the earliest surviving British film scenario, this was written and filmed in late November or early December 1901. With these few pencilled notes as a guide, Mitchell and Kenyon filmed Percy Honri as 'Mr Moon' grim-

Concordia: Scenes from 'The Demon Woods', 'The Man in the Moon' and 'The Awakening'

acing through a circular hole cut in a piece of plywood covered with black velvet. Grandpa cut out the tiny banjo with a fretsaw, and strung it up to animate the 'business' he wanted filmed. Now preserved in the archives of the British Film Institute, it is the sole surviving example of the Blackburn pioneers' work. As his 11 January 1902 *Era* advertisement indicated, Percy's new act at the 'Pav' incorporated scenic effects by W. T. Hemsley and introduced '...the Greatest Cinematograph Novelty of the Age (Copyright) Oh! Mister Moon!'.

Later, to cover an awkward costume change in his show *Concordia*, he used film again for the amusing 'Quick Change Dressing Room' actually filmed by Charles Urban on one of his Urban Bioscope cameras at George Hana's studio in Bedford Street. In the film, Percy has no less than three dressers 'helping' him to change – his father, George Hana and his assistant. This film is also preserved by the B.F.I. My father describes Urban thus:

> ... a man of large cigars, enormous energy and magnetic personality. He had a great enthusiasm for using film for education, natural history, science and travel and what later came to be called documentary films. . . . Percy Honri knew him well, often meeting him at music halls in London and Brighton, occasionally participating in Urban's bioscope activities. . . . Charles Urban was a business man and a technician, who justified the motto embodied in his trade mark 'We put the world before you'. He did this not only by the promotion of routine films, but in the first organisation for regularly reporting world events. The first purpose-built building for film organisation in Wardour Street was at No. 89 'Urbanora House' with a studio on the top floor, film processing and equipment stores below and a theatre on the ground floor. Meanwhile, the rest of the 'trade' carried on in Cecil Court, Charing Cross Road or Leicester Square . . . .

In 1905, with George Albert Smith, Urban evolved the first successful 'natural' colour system – the Urban Smith Kinemacolour two-colour film system, which used two-colour filters on both the film cameras and projectors, and ran at double speed.

Percy Honri accomplished another first at the Euston Music Hall in March 1909, when he commissioned Foulsham and Banfield to take moving pictures as well as stills of *Concordia* for use as a 'trailer'. These were the very first film scenes shot in a real music hall. But whilst their 'stills' compared favourably with the earlier 'Photos by Hana', the trailer did not satisfy Grandpa; it was never used and has not survived.

Just five weeks before the outbreak of war in 1914, G. B. Samuelson's new 'kinematograph studio' at Worton Hall, Isleworth, was officially opened by Vesta Tilley – who 'cut the tape guarding the entrance to what is claimed to be the finest studio in the world with a pair of golden scissors which being superstitious she bought with a customary coin'. The enterprising Bertie Samuelson had also persuaded the music hall magnate Walter de Frece, who later married Vesta Tilley, to propose a toast of success to a British Film Producing Company: 'It might appear that I am going back on myself in proposing success to a kinema company when my money is invested in theatres and music halls – but as a matter of fact I believe that the picture theatres are merely educating the public for other forms of entertainment . . . .' The veteran film producer Will Barker emphasised this point further when he spoke of having persuaded Tree to be filmed as 'Henry VIII' because 'the pictures are making audiences for the legitimate stage. . .'. Tree insisted that the celluloid versions of the His Majesty's Theatre stage production were to be destroyed after only six weeks' showing, and further that only twenty prints of the film were made, ten for London and ten for provincial presentation. Sir Herbert knew that film sold and hired in the open market was used for months, and in the days before the advent of safety film and techniques of protective coatings, soon became scratched and covered with oil and dirt. So Will Barker 'duly applied a match to the twenty copies of highly inflammable nitrate film at the impressive ceremonial burning before a large group of pressmen and theatricals in the ground of his Ealing Studios . . . ' – and whilst the letter of contract was upheld honourably, students of theatre and film history have lost a unique example of Tree's style.

It was in 1914, too, that Joseph Wilkinson, secretary to the Incorporated Association of Kinematograph Manufacturers, told the Nicholson Committee at the House of Commons that ' . . . there were now in this country, 43 publishers of films; 200 firms who were engaged in the business of renting films, and the number of picture theatres was about 5,000. . . '.

Three years later Percy Honri had a trailer filmed for his single act, but this time he went to Cecil Hepworth's studio at Walton-on-Thames, and took his son who was movie-mad to watch Hepworth direct. This is how my father remembers that day, and 'The Affair of the Static Lens Cap':

' . . . It was made about the time Alma Taylor was making *Merely Mrs Stubbs* with Henry Edwards. . . . The way they used to do things then – Cecil Hepworth would say: "Well, Mr Honri – what scene would you like?" and Father said: "I'd like a country house with some stairs so I can make an entrance."

'"While you're making up, we'll have the stage set."

'And he got the stage manager, who was the art director as well you might say. He'd get some stage hands to bring some stock sets out – and within half an hour, there was the set, palms and all that – armchairs. He paid Hepworth twenty pounds and one shilling a foot for the print. As a trailer it ran about 200 feet. . . .

' . . . They had a rehearsal, and he came down and did like an entrance and started playing. Now Hepworth was very very keen on always having the lens of the camera capped to stop dust getting on the front – so whenever the lens wasn't in use, it used to be capped. At the end of the take I was stood near the camera, and I said to Mr Hepworth:

'"Mr Hepworth, I don't think he took the cap off the lens when he was

Top, Baynham Honri operates
the radio transmitter for the first
broadcast from a moving train,
'The Flying Scotsman'; far left,
with his Moy camera on board
R.M.S. Berengaria 1922; as
President of the British
Kinematograph Society 1953

doing that scene!" So Mr Hepworth instantly came forward and said:

'"Mr Honri – Mr Honri – we'll just have another take of that – just to make sure...." This time Mr Hepworth looked at the cameraman as if he could kill him....'

Royal Thompson Trio, programme and songsheet front cover

COPE'S CIGARETTES.
29.—Hetty King.

COPE'S CIGARETTES.
2.—Gus Elen.

COPE'S CIGARETTES.
4.—Joe Elvin.

COPE'S CIGARETTES.
20.—Tom Costello.

COPE'S CIGARETTES.
28.—Alexandra Dagmar.

COPE'S CIGARETTES.
6.—George Robey.

COPE'S CIGARETTES.
35.—Percy Honri.

COPE'S CIGARETTES.
37.—Neil Kenyon.

COPE'S CIGARETTES.
17.—Eugene Stratton.

COPE'S CIGARETTES.
41.—George Bastow.

COPE'S CIGARETTES.
19.—G. H. Chirgwin.

COPE'S CIGARETTES
45.—Poluski Bros.

6 · WE GET INVOLVED

'HERE Percy – got your concertina handy? This is that parody of mine I was telling you about. Wal Pink wants a whole lot of 'em to use on handbills for the pickets.'

Percy and Gus Elen were both members of the year old Variety Artistes Federation, and had just heard that the Adney Payne halls were now involved in the strike that had begun the previous day, Monday 21 January 1907, at the Gibbons houses. The V.A.F., as part of the National Alliance of performers, stage staff and musicians, had now come out at the fourteen London music halls controlled by George Adney Payne and his son-in-law Walter Gibbons.

The dressing room at the Paragon soon filled up as the sound of the concertina carried down the corridors. Some of Joe Elvin's *Forester's Day* company squeezed in with Joe himself, Marie Kendall and her husband Steve McCarthy, the eighteen year old Gertie Gitana and a few others:

'Let's be hearing it, Gus ... we can't wait all night, that's the second ad lib Percy's played.'

Gus Elen stood up on a chair, and struck an attitude; the banter continued and Percy blew the wind out of his concertina –

'Careful Percy – we can't blow Gus back to the Canterbury or on to the Oxford till we've heard his masterpiece – can we?' shouted Marie as she balanced herself against Gus's chair. So Gus began to sing:

> Some people visit halls where the artistes are on strike,
> But I ain't one of them not me;
> If a fellow starts to fight for his freedom and for right,
> I'm going to back him up d'ye see.
> I'm going to help the strikers put the Trust upon the rocks,
> And they're bound to win, no matter who says nay,
> For it makes no odds to me
> What the dividends will be

Reading left to right from top:
Joe Elvin; Hackney street
scene © *GLC*; Tom Webster
cartoon 1908; Gus Elen; Gertie
Gitana; Little Tich

Give the strikers their just claims is what I say. . .
For what's the use of going in a show
   If there ain't no stars about;
For yer can't give a show if the bands and staff
   And the artistes all come out.
If yer don't get stars,
   The public stop out;
That's a' argyment what's sensible and sound;
Get yer stars back; pay your bandsmen;
Treat your staff a bit more handsome;
Or your dividends will never come round.'

Through the applause and cheers greeting the parody, Percy modulated into one of his own, and sang:

Rule Britannia, Britannia rules the waves.
Two shows every night and six matinees.

'Well, that's to the point – and after all we do know the tune.' That was Marie's comment. 'Steve – how does Whit Cunliffe's parody go?' With a smile, Steve McCarthy picks up a silver-topped cane from the corner of the dressing room, and begins the Cunliffe, strut, so far as space allows: 'All right, Percy?'

Hello, Hello, Hello,
It's the Music Hall Strike again.
It's not the stars
   Who are feeling the jars,
It's the poor little pro
   We're helping, you know.
Hello, hello, hello,
The way to help is plain,
Don't visit the show of Henri Gros,
Gibbons or Adney Payne.

With a final twirl of the cane, Steve took a 'call': 'Did you hear the one about the Sister act at the Canterbury – one was feeling very poorly: "Had any pain, Lily?" Lily replied tearfully: "No, it was one of the other directors. . .".'
But not all had 'struck' at the Paragon, as *The Stage* reported:

   . . . A large crowd had assembled both inside and outside of the house. The pickets at the stage door were Messrs F. Parker (of the Gottams) Charles Butler, Harry Mansfield and George Sinclair (of Sincloair & Parr) and their efforts were unremitting. Inside the house the audience waited patiently while the full orchestra under Mr Arthur Grimmett played several selections. But the house was ill-lighted and understaffed, the majority of stagehands having joined the movement and there were no company to appear. After some waiting Mr Charles Beecham, the manager, appeared before the curtain and explained matters. He would offer no personal opinion on the strike, he said, but thought those old stage hands and others who had failed them had treated them very shabbily, Mr Adney Payne being a very fair and considerate employer. He thanked Mr Arthur Grimmett and the band for their staunchness and announced that performances would be given after that night as usual with an emergency company.

The audience then quietly left the house, their money being returned to them at the various box offices. The artists who were billed to appear were Joe Elvin & Co in *Forester's Day*, Marie Kendall, Percy Honri, Nellie Wallace, Jaeger & Jaeger, Tom Leamore, Howe & Ardie, Steve MacCarthy, Millie Payne, Les Grisses, Gertie Gitana, Lottie Collins, Sylvia De Barry, Price & Revost and Wilson Hallett.

It was the same tale over at the Canterbury where many of the Paragon bill were doubling.

In that same issue of 24 January, *The Stage*'s editorial indicated that it ranged itself with the performers:

> ... Subsequent remarkable developments show how sharp the conflict between employers and employed has become. It is a thousand pities that managers should not, as we urged them the other week, have entered into friendly negotiations.
>
> They probably counted on the easy-going nature of artists. In that they have been completely mistaken; and they are now face to face with a most formidable combination, which has practically the power to shut their houses and enlist the masses of the public against them. ... We can find nothing unreasonable in what the artists ask for themselves. The modified Barring Clause – One mile and Three months in Town, Five miles and Five months in the Provinces, the half salary for matinees. ... We sympathise with the artists in their grievances as much as we admire them for the example of organisation, espirit de corps and fine loyalty to each other that, from highest to lowest, they have set.

The Era, in its coverage of the dispute in its 26 January issue, seems to lean towards the managers in its review of the scratch programme at the Oxford:

> ... An attenuated orchestra took their seats, under the direction of Mr Burgess, and Mr Blyth-Pratt came to the front of the curtain and said:
>
> "You are aware, ladies and gentlemen, of what is taking place, and I am sorry to tell you that the Variety Artistes Federation is endeavouring to prevent our artists working here tonight. I regret that it will be quite impossible to give our regular programme, but I am going to put forward an entertainment which I hope will really entertain you."
>
> Among the entertainers announced by the manager were Mrs Brown-Potter, who gave a recitation; Mr Tom Clare, entertainer at the piano;

Mr Ted Thomas, who sang a jockey song; Mr Jan Rudenyi; Mlle D'Aubigny, from the Paris Opera House, who sang Tosti's 'Good-bye' with much taste; the Hungarian violinist, who played a rhapsody; a diminutive Continental mandolinist, a decidedly good player, accompanied by a buxom vocalist; and a very welcome turn was supplied by Corman's Juveniles, who kept the show going with choruses, dancing and ballads, the turn winding up with a gavotte in Watteau costumes, which fetched the house immensely. A very agreeable impression was caused by the appearance of Mrs George Adney Payne, who returned to the stage temporarily to assist her husband in the crisis. Looking particularly winsome in a simple white evening dress, Mrs Payne, who bravely overcame her nervousness, sang with much fervour and culture 'The Holy City' and 'Dear Heart'. A couple of comic acrobats were also included in the scratch programme and a comic singer. The audience behaved admirably, and were manifestly fair in their attitude, and applauded without stint when such recognition was deserved.

There was at least one unpleasant altercation between one of the Chartists and the manager, and we are given to understand that a very conspicuous and important member of the V.A.F. left the saloon at the request of one of the directors; but, taking into consideration the excitement prevailing, both parties displayed admirable control. The directors who arrived about ten o'clock included Messrs George Adney Payne, Henry Tozer, Henry Sutton, Walter Gibbons, Joseph Davis and Henri Gros, the last-mentioned gentleman being called up from the country, where he had been recuperating after a severe illness. The saloon, too, was largely filled by artists and agents, among whom we noticed Messrs G. and F. Peel, Sydney Hyman, Sydney L. Cohen, Edward Granville, Harry Day, Emanuel Warner, Jack Somers, Ernest Edelsten, Didcott, and Howell. Mr and Mrs Gus Elen came in to see the show, and among the artists also present were Mr Edgar and Miss Claire Romaine, Mr Bert Clark, and Miss Hamilton, Mr Barney Armstrong, Joe O'Gorman, and others. . . .

The Performer, as the official organ of the V.A.F., was quite naturally for the performers, and some of the reports of the various 'closures' make entertaining reading:

Holborn Empire. At this hall Mgr Gibbons made his grand stand play. About twenty agents were in at the first show Monday, and the way they hustled was a sight to see, for in time of trouble agents must 'stand in' just as artistes must 'stand out'. Telephone bells were ringing, and hurry calls were flying, and one would have thought the town was on fire from the way they stirred around. . . .

A solitary pianist sat down and played a selection from the 'Belle of New York'. Then a pretty young lady sang 'Good-bye', and, to tell the truth, it looked like what she sang. More tinkling from the piano, and then a white moving picture sheet showed 'The Alps seen through a Telescope'. After hard work a very odd show indeed got down to the final 'King' and no attempt was made to give a second show. Outside policemen were as thick as hops. . . . Tuesday, Jan. 22. Mr George Adney Payne entered into negotiations with the Alliance, and asked for a postponement and second meeting; but in the meantime Mr Payne wrote to the musicians and staff telling them he would not recognise the Alliance, or any of the Societies composing it. He further tried to induce Mr MacNaghten to break his agreement with the Alliance; he also assisted Mr Gibbons with musicians, staff and artistes. As he threw down the gauntlet, the challenge was accepted. An ultimatum, expiring at 4 p.m. Tuesday Jan 22 was sent to Mr Payne, but the Alliance receiving no reply to same, a strike was ordered at 4.15 which made a total of 14 halls affected. The result of the ultimatum upon the halls in question is given below:

Paragon. Everybody out at 7.45. Orchestra played but no artistes appeared. Money returned. Somebody pinched the key of the electrical switchboard, and there will be no 'fiat lux' till it is found. Canterbury. No show. The sponge was thrown up at 7.45, and the Canterbury is hushed and still as the Canterbury Cathedral. South London. Closed down at 7.45 . . . Tivoli. Though right in the heart of London, in the middle of the teeming Strand, this house was utterly unable to put on a show. No orchestra present. Pictures put on until the people began to get sick of them. A fat lady who was late arriving said to her husband: 'George, why is it whenever you take me to a show up in London it is always time for letting out?' Oxford . . . One of the performers was recognised as a recent 'bar tender' . . . Hippodrome Ealing. Here the fond plans of Mr Gibbons melted like a snowball in perdition. No band, no performers, no performance. The proud musical director wouldn't even play the piano. Empress Brixton. Not affected. Director Grimes having signed Charter on Monday Jan 21. Hippodrome Putney. Also not affected, being under the same management as the Empress. Metropolitan. Not affected. Henri Gros ill. We are fighting fair and according to the rules. No mean advantages. Empire Chelsea. Management of Henri Gros. Same case. . . .

Not even the pictures or the elephants could save the managerial face, as William Payne, manager of the South London, was to find out as he walked to centre stage: 'You've had the elephants on once, and the pictures once. Would you care to have the pictures again or the elephants?' The audience gave a terrific howl of 'No!'

'Elephants?' (Yes!! yes – yes).

'Very well, we will put on the elephants again.'

So Lockhart's Elephants lumbered back on stage to repeat their routine. But they were no sooner before the footlights than they were booed and called 'BLACKLEGS!!!'

COBORN – FATHER OF THE PERFORMERS' UNION

The seeds of the 1907 dispute went back many years, and had grown as the links

Lockhart's Elephants

'Performer' cartoon 1906
illustrating the fears of music
hall artistes

Variety Artistes' Federation.

APPLICATION FORM.

Surname *O'Gorman*

Christian Name *Joe*

Male or Female *Man*

If over 21 years of age

Line of Business

Permanent Address *75, Clapham Road, Brixton, S.*
(Where a Letter will always find)

If Member of a Troupe, give

Proposed by

Seconded by

I wish to become a Member of the V.A.F. and herewith enclose 2s. 6d. as entrance fee, and agree to pay the weekly Subscription of 6d. on demand. If elected I promise to observe all the Rules and Regulations of the V.A.F.

Signed *Joe O'Gorman*

All Entrance Fees and Donations to be forwarded to :—

Mr. W. H. McCARTHY,
Hon. Treasurer (pro tem.),
Vaudeville Club,
98, Charing Cross Road,
London, W.C.

Mason & Bart
P.A. – 97, Brixton Road,
London, S.W.9.
'Phone – Brixton 1043.

Vacancies :—

Joe O'Gorman's V.A.F. application form: Member No. 1; Harry Mason, V.A.F. founder member; first ever photograph of the Water Rats 1890, showing (left to right from top) Geo. Beauchamp, Geo. Sinclair, Geo. Fairburn, Joe Tennyson, Frank Travis, Andrew Weatherly, Arthur Forrest, Geo Harris, Joe O'Gorman, John Collinson, H. M. Edmund, Fred Griffiths, Joe Griffiths, Geo. Loyal, Will Oliver, Chas. Wallace, Fred Eplett, Wal Pink, Joe Elvin, Harry Freeman, John Lotto, Fred Harvey, Dan Leno, Tom Brantford

between the circuits, syndicates and trusts of the managers had become stronger. This strike was unique because there were no clear-cut demarcation lines between employer and employee – many performers were employers themselves, and even shareholders. Many managers admitted there was a case for negotiation, and some, like MacNaghten and Grimes, even accepted the National Alliance Charter.

As far back as 1885, Charlie Coborn had formed the Music Hall Artistes Association, the first performers' union, to combat a move by the Managers Association, of issuing a list of named artistes and their salary rates. If a manager exceeded those rates, he was liable to a £50 fine. In his autobiography *The Man who broke the Bank*, Coborn relates with pride the story of how the union was formed in the billiards room of a pub, hired for two hours at a shilling an hour, and chaired by Joe Keegan, father of Joe Elvin, one of the founders of the Grand Order of Water Rats.

> The cover was put on the billiard table and we all signed our names on a sheet of foolscap paper. Not long after, that sheet of paper went a-missing, but what would I not give to have it now! ... The name of the public house was 'The Red Lion', and, though it has been greatly improved and altered, the dear old clock still smiles out upon the world, as though proud of the fact that beneath it on that day was formed and started the first Trade Union of the Stage.

It had originally been arranged to hold the meeting at the Trocadero Music Hall where Charlie was appearing for Robert Bignell, but under pressure from the Managers Association Bignell was forced to withdraw permission previously granted for his hall to be used. In his book, Coborn goes on to say: 'although a a lifelong Conservative, I am and always have been an ardent Trades Unionist. I hate tyranny, whether exercised by an individual or a combination, but union amongst fellow-workers in their common interest must be always a desirable state of affairs.... Having been chiefly instrumental in starting a trade union amongst artistes, it will be readily understood that I was not exactly *persona grata* with the various managers....' Charlie Coborn's enthusiasm and energy never waned even if, as he writes, he did not 'get very much help or sympathy from my own side'. One of his supporters was my great-grandfather Harry Thompson, who wrote in December 1888 the following letter to *The Era*:

> Music Hall Combination. To the Editor of The Era. Sir – Having read a letter in the current issue of The Era from Mr Charles Coborn on the subject of co-operation amongst music hall artists, it seems to me that an easy solution of the difficulty could be found if a few influential members of the profession would call a meeting in London for the purpose of considering the matter; a committee could then be formed and the necessary steps taken for our protection.
>
> Managers have commenced an aggressive policy, and it remains for us to combat their efforts to practically boycott the profession. The lowest

ARGYLE THEATRE,
BIRKENHEAD.

Sole Proprietor and Manager - - - - - - - D. J. CLARKE.

CONTRACT.

An Agreement made the ....21st....... day of ....August.........191.7...

BETWEEN ....D. J. Clarke.........hereinafter called the management of the one part, and

...........Percy Honri.

9227.

EXCLUSIVE WEST-END ENGAGEMENT.

31.3.08

LONDON THEATRES OF VARIETIES, LIMITED.

Offices:—HOLBORN EMPIRE OFFICES, HIGH HOLBORN, W.C. 1

An Agreement made the 18th day of April 191 8 between LONDON THEATRES OF VARIETIES LIMITED (hereinafter called the Management) of the one part and Percy Honri (hereinafter called the Artiste) of the other part **Witnesseth** that the Management hereby engages the Artiste and the Artiste accepts an engagement to appear as Concertinist (or in his usual entertainment)

Percy Honri's touring company *1915 Revue* at Euston Station; *1917* Argyle Theatre, Birkenhead and *1918* Palladium contracts (details)

class of workmen have their trades' unions; why then, cannot we, who work with our brains, organise a system to carry out the same policy on slightly different lines?

Proprietors should remember that if we depend on them for 'the ghost', so they look to us for 'talent'. If the one ceases to exist the other dies. Capital and labour are, and always will be, dependent on each other, and the sooner managers recognise the fact the better for them and for us. There can be no question, as Mr Coborn fears, of quarrelling with proprietors, and his very apt quotation is perfectly correct; but managers must consider their 'bread and butter' also. Without our assistance they cannot live, nor we without them. They have combined; let us do the same. . . .

Gus Elen referred to the 'one sidedness' of most house contracts in his letter published in *The Era* on 25 June 1887:

Music Hall Engagements.
Sir – Some eight months ago I signed an engagement to open Monday next (June 27th) at a provincial music hall, and I sent in a week ago 'matter for bill' in the usual way, and had arranged everything for my departure from London. I have just received at last moment the following telegram: 'Shall not expect you; business bad.' And I am to be thrown out like this! I think there ought to be something done for artistes in this plight. If you sue a proprietor you can rest assured you are booked then for a later date – and very late too. If engagements were made out to this effect, that artistes should receive the salary agreed on their engagement, perform or not, providing that the proprietor does not warn them a month previous to their opening of his intention to close – in case of fire, etc. it is of course a different thing – the profession then would have fair play. . . .

But the support for Charlie's schemes remained incidental. Many other Benefit Societies sprang up to gain the corporate interests of pros and Charlie Coborn's Music Hall Artistes Association with its emphasis on trade unionism soon faded away.

In February 1897, Dan Leno, Eugene Stratton and C. Douglas Stuart, founder and editor of *The Encore*, formed the Music Hall Railway Rates Association which was able to obtain for performers rail fares at three-quarters of the normal rate, the same concession Stuart had secured for the legitimate theatre from the railway companies the previous year. Until the nationalisation of the railways this arrangement stood for the pros' inevitable Sunday train journey. There were lower rates for 'Theatrical Baggage' too, and 'turns' would use these to travel 'skips', props, stage cloths and often personal items as well. I still recall Grandpa sending us an old motor mower on theatrical rate! The M.H.R.R.A. extended beyond 'three-quarters fares', into legal assistance and the question of equitable contracts between performers and proprietors. At the London Pavilion in 1900, a form of contract applicable to London and the provinces was agreed to by one hundred and fifty managers and there seemed to be grounds for hope that a standard contract would come into universal use. But the M.H.R.R.A. rested on its sleepers, and the Grand Order of Water Rats, representing as it did then the leading performers of the day, began to flex its muscles. Encouraged by George Gray, the 1905 Annual General Meeting of the M.H.R.R.A. executive committee was virtually 'taken over' by the Water Rats.

The time was now ripe for the creation of a new and lasting trade union in that fiercely individual world of music hall – the lone voices had gathered support in the various professional bodies, and after a series of joint meetings (many held at the Vaudeville Club in Charing Cross Road), on 18 February 1906 the Variety Artistes Federation was founded and registered as Trade Union No. 1378. The fifteen founder members came equally from the Water Rats, the Music Hall Railway Rates Association and the London branch of the International Artistes Lodge. They were C. C. Bartram, Harry Blake, W. H. Clemart, John D'Osta, James Forman, Frank Gerald, Fred Herbert, William Lee, Joe O'Gorman, Harry Mason, Charles Pastor, Wal Pink, Max Rose, Fred Russell and Albert Schafer. By 21 January 1907, the V.A.F.'s roll of membership numbered 3,799 and the union had its own penny weekly, *The Performer*. Sixty years later, in May 1967 the V.A.F. was incorporated in British Equity – the era of pigeon-holing the different aspects of the performing arts had come to an end. It was a proud day for me as a member of the Equity Council to welcome Jimmy Edwards, last in the line of V.A.F. chairmen that began with Joe O'Gorman, to the new joint body.

'– WHILE THE IRON IS HOT!'

How and why did the 1907 strike happen? The V.A.F., in concert with N.A.T.E. (National Association of Theatrical Employees) and the A.M.U. (Amalgamated Musicians Union) had presented the managers with the 'Charter of the National Alliance'. In it were the minimum conditions demanded by the constituent unions of the Alliance. For the A.M.U. these were a 36 shilling London minimum per instrumentalist plus pro rata half salary for each matinee at twice-nightly houses. Full salary was to be payable for matinees at once-nightly halls. The N.A.T.E. demands were more complicated, but for 'Daymen in the Stage, Flies, Property and Gas Departments', the minimum demanded was 24 shillings a week exclusive of show-money (for twice-nightly houses this was 2s 6d per night and 2s per matinee plus overtime). This was for a five-day week. The V.A.F.'s demands set out no minima but stated that all matinees should be paid at the rate of one-twelfth salary for each matinee; that no artiste should be transferred from one hall to another without his consent; that 'time' should not be varied after Monday without the artiste's consent; that the V.A.F. form of contract should be adopted as soon as supplied; that no commission should be stopped on direct bookings; that the 'barring clause' should be modified to one mile and three months; and that all disputes should be referred to a board of arbitration of two managers and two artistes plus an independent chairman.

The first music hall managers to consider the Charter were Frank MacNaghten, Walter Gibbons and George Adney Payne. On 9 January 1907, MacNaghten, controller of eight provincial and five London halls, signed an agreement with the National Alliance. But as Frank Gerald, secretary of the V.A.F., reported to the first mass meeting of the Alliance held at the Surrey Theatre on Sunday 20 January, Mr Gibbons said 'I am a beaten man; I do not want it to go to the public that you wiped the floor with me. Do not ask me to sign any agreement; I will give you my word of honour.' *The Performer* reported thus:

> By an ultimatum sent Mgr Gibbons on Saturday, he was given until four o'clock Monday 21 January to append his autograph to our Charter. Florists have flowers called "Four o'clocks" because they blossom at that hour in the afternoon; but sad to say the affirmation of Gibbons did not burst into blossom at that hour. At 5.15 p.m. the Alliance Committee called out all V.A.F., A.M.U. and N.A.T.E. members at all of Gibbons' halls. On the Tuesday, when the strike had spread to the Adney Payne halls as well, the Tivoli manager received the following telegrams from his two 'bill-toppers':
> I AM LEARNING A NEW CORNET SOLO. CANNOT TEAR MYSELF AWAY – LITTLE TICH.
> I AM BUSY PUTTING A NEW FLOUNCE ON MY DRESS SO I CANNOT APPEAR TONIGHT – MARIE LLOYD.

Soon an Emergency Relief Fund for the 'wines and spirits' was started by Little Tich, Arthur Roberts and Joe Elvin, to which hundreds of members and sympathisers subscribed. Hosts of pros undertook picket duties at the 'barred' halls, and a few, including Marie Kendall and her husband Steve McCarthy, were arrested for obstruction.

At their second mass meeting at the Surrey, Frank Gerald announced that Dr Distin Maddick, owner of the Scala Theatre, had agreed that 'La Scala shall be the home of the music hall profession in England'. *The Performer* trumpeted the news that

> ... we have taken the Scala Theatre which is within a few yards of the Oxford. Here we shall get to close quarters with our enemies and endeavour to prove to them that Talent and Ability constitute the most important factors of success in the Variety World. ... An industrial strike can in no way be compared to our dispute, for when ordinary workmen 'come out' they are compelled to leave the machinery and the raw materials behind them. But we, the Artistes and Musicians, can never be in such a position as that, for when we strike we take the machinery and the raw materials with us, to use and to sell as suit our purpose best. The managers cannot replace the talent they have lost.

The managers did try to replace the stars that had struck – many a third-rate turn found that 'strike-breaking' for his or her West End music hall debut was not an enjoyable occupation, as music hall pickets were something to reckon with for pithy comment. Even the Salvation Army bands refused to play for the managers. By 7 February, the situation had hardened somewhat – Oswald Stoll, speaking of the Charter, had said 'I must ignore it' – the Alliance put on shows at the 'Horns', Kennington, and 'The Myddelton Hall', Islington, and prepared for the Gala show at the Scala. *The Performer* published dozens of advertisements of support from members working in the provinces, together with columns of subscribers to the Relief Fund and the names of the 'blackleg' artistes.

Two days later, on 9 February, the managers via their London Entertainments Protection Association officially recognised the National Alliance! With the advice of the London Trades Council, and in particular of the dockers' leader, Ben Tillett, negotiations continued. The day after the National Alliance's own show at the Scala had opened – Tuesday 13 February – an armistice was declared pending the unconditional arbitration of George R. Askwith, K. C., the Board of Trade arbitrator; this meant the withdrawal of legal actions on the managers' side, and of the pickets by the Alliance. Acting on Shakespeare's injunction 'Hang out our banners on the outward walls', the Vaudeville Club put out a banner with thirty-inch letters: 'PEACE! ALL THE STARS RETURN TO THE HALLS TO-NIGHT.'

Whilst the silver and copper tinkled once more into the box offices, the performers, musicians and stage staff confidently awaited the outcome of the arbitration tribunal. The lesson of the strike was that performers learned to think less of self-interest and more of mutual co-operation. They discovered that a combination of talent can secure fairer and better conditions than individual talent. Percy Honri and his father (who was V.A.F. branch chairman at Ashton-under-Lyne) believed that firmly, whilst his father-in-law and brother-in-law Willie 'on t'other side o' fence' accepted it.

MARIE LLOYD VERBATIM

Legend has it that ' the halls' struck in their hundreds – in fact just under 300 performers, 213 musicians and 90 stage employees were 'on strike' during the twenty-four-day music hall war. Arbitration proceedings lasted twenty-three days during April and early May, and on 14 June 1907 G. R. Askwith, K. C., made his award – which went a long way towards the demands of the Alliance. The transcript of the evidence given before the arbitrator runs to over 600,000 words. Marie Lloyd gave her evidence on Wednesday 10 April in this way, parrying the questions of Walter Payne representing the Entertainments Protection Association:

W.P. Have you an engagement at the Oxford at the present time?
M.L. Have I?
W.P. Yes?
M.L. Yes.
W.P. Can you tell me what your salary is?
M.L. You ought to know, it is there.

Faithfully yours
George Formby
1916.

Yours very Sincerely
Vesta Victoria

W.P. I cannot find it, and that is why I am asking you!

M.L. Eighty pounds.

W.P. That is for the one hall?

M.L. That is for the one hall, and I am worth five hundred pounds.

W.P. Do you remember being there in 1903 at a salary of sixty pounds a week?

M.L. Yes.

W.P. And in 1900 at a salary of fourty pounds?

M.L. Yes.

W.P. And in 1896 at twenty-five?

M.L. Yes; and in 1889 at four pounds. That shows how I have improved!

W.P. . . . Well now, I will just take one week – the week ending 3 February 1906, you were at the Canterbury at sixty pounds, at the Tivoli at fifty-five pounds, and at Camberwell?

M.L. Yes.

W.P. The Camberwell salary I have not got. So that in that week, may I take it that your total salary was somewhere about a hundred and fifty pounds on turns?

M.L. 'A lot of money, ain't it Bill?' That is what I earned. Shall I tell you what I had to spend to get that?

W.P. I would rather you did not!

M.L. You should see some of my little bills. Will you tell me now, then, how many months I was off last year?

W.P. I do not quite know.

M.L. Ah! and my expenses going on just the same.

W.P. It was not because you could not get an engagement, was it?

M.L. No, that was illness; but they do not send me anything on Saturday if I do not earn it.

Marie Lloyd's sense of comedy is never far away as she answers Charles Doughty, the V.A.F. counsel.

C.D. Out of this hundred and fifty pounds my friend was mentioning for turn money, what would your expenses come to?

M.L. About a hundred and forty-nine pounds.

C.D. Cannot you be a little more accurate than that?

M.L. I will have to give it to the income tax people. I do not want to be worried too soon with that. I will tell you what I will do. I will go on for nothing a week if you will give me £10 a week, and you can take my salary and lay it out for me. Now, then, that is what I get out of it.

On contracts Marie was very pragmatic: 'Supposing you had all the contracts worded alike, and you were paying a person a very large salary, and you thought they ought to be barred, you would simply write that in. Then if the artiste signed it there it is; it is pointed out to him. It is not put in tiny words, like some of the contracts are that want a telescope to find them.'

T. E. Dunville

MR. MARK SHERIDAN.

Mark Sheridan

Two further awards were made in 1913 and in 1919, which took into account the many changes that came about in variety. In a letter written to my grandfather in January 1926, his brother-in-law P. B. Broadhead, leader of the 'independent managers', shrewdly observed:

> ... I know now on reading through the script of your revue that like many more you yearn for the old happy music hall days when work was plentiful and things were good. Who killed the Music Hall? Who crowed after the last two Arbitrations over what they had wrung from the Managers? — Chorus of young and old, thin and fat chanticleers 'Cock-a-doodle do — we rule the roost etc'. And who has now beautiful Awards and empty date books? — Those blind chanticleers. And who laid low and found other forms of entertainment to fill their programme? ...

In April 1972, Alan Plater, writer of many T.V. plays, invited me to advise him in a play he was writing for the B.B.C. *The Edwardians* series produced by Mark Shivas. It was about the 1907 music hall strike, and Alan called it *The Reluctant Juggler*. The play was directed by Brian Farnham and designed by Peter Seddon; and the entire show was shot on location at Wilton's Music Hall. Alan wrote a warm human script that was in 'period'; none of his characters was allowed to be self-indulgent, and he had the great original songs of the stars which were skilfully woven into the story of pros who remained true to their roots. Alan Plater has been kind enough to let me quote from part of a dressing room scene from *The Reluctant Juggler*. Two of the stars are discussing audiences and another performer — a frequent dressing room topic. The stars are George Formby and Vesta Victoria, and this is how Alan describes it:

INT. DRESSING ROOM. NIGHT

(A QUIET, GENTLE SCENE. GEORGE AND VESTA JUST CHATTING – EACH HAS A GLASS OF THE HARD STUFF BUT NO SUGGESTION OF A BOOZING SESSION, JUST SOCIABLE LIKE)

GEORGE: Oh aye, I'd go on strike tomorrow if they asked me.

VESTA: Would you?

GEORGE: Well, I mean to say ... what a life, isn't it? Saturday night, you finish last house in Portsmouth or Southampton and you look into your diary to see where to next. And it says Aberdeen. You know?

(PAUSE)

Sundays, sat in trains ...

VESTA: Always plenty of good company.

GEORGE: Yes but even in a crowd you're on your own really, aren't you?

VESTA: You *are* in a bad way, dear, aren't you? You'll be going the way of Dan Leno ...

GEORGE: Oh aye, well I've got me Hamlet set hanging behind the door you know ...

VESTA: Anyway, you're getting well paid, aren't you?

GEORGE: (MOCK INNOCENCE) Oh, are they supposed to pay you? I thought it was just for goodwill, like . . .
(PAUSE)
Mind, it's nice when they shout and cheer.

VESTA: They need something to cheer about, most of them . . .

GEORGE: But there was this feller on the bill tonight . . . juggler . . .

VESTA: I know him. Misery.

GEORGE: They never cheer him. He's not bad . . . clever . . . I can't do what he does . . . but they don't cheer him . . . bit of clapping like, for decency's sake . . . and he's getting on, he won't get no better. I mean one day, mebbe quite soon, they'll stop clapping him altogether . . . then what?

VESTA: That can happen to any of us.

GEORGE: Oh aye, I know that right enough . . .

VESTA: And when it does, well what's the odds? You just look back and remember the time when they cheered and shouted. There's still only a few of us. Most people never get clapped and cheered at all . . . we've got *that* you see . . . .

'THE VERDICT WAS . . .'

. . . I earned my living as a funny man. Can you imagine what it means to a funny man to find that his jokes don't go? Can you imagine what it meant for me to stand waiting in the wings for my number to go up, trembling all over with fear and fright, and then to face the public that used to roar with delight, and get a few scattered hands? Oh, those awful nights! The crowd, no longer my friends, who struck matches and talked. The look of pity on the face of the conductor, and the few words from the stage-door man when I crept away: 'Never mind, Mr Dany; can't always knock 'em, y'know.'

How close to the truth are those few sentences from Cosmo Hamilton's short story *Lame dogs* written in 1912.

That is the dilemma of the performer. He values his independence and yet his audience is his lifeline. No one asks you to be a pro, so you learn to adapt, to work 'horses for courses' — or you leave the business. Your television screens are full of performers who became 'overnight' successes over ten thousand nights. Perhaps many a pro's hopes and fears can be expressed in this gag of Max Wall's: 'Last week I followed a conjuror — half way through my act they started hissing the conjuror again!'

The knife-edge between success and failure is part of the challenge presented to the performer at every single performance, and especially does this apply to comics. It has been this mental strain and anguish that has destroyed so many talents, even topliners like Mark Sheridan and T. E. Dunville were driven to a desperate end.

Top, Percy Honri on stage
1950; right, M. R. Mitchell's
portrait of Percy Honri

The week of 17 March 1924, found Dunville topping the bill with Gertie Gitana at the Clapham Grand; he played both houses on the Monday and Tuesday, but never appeared Wednesday. On the Saturday, his body was found in Caversham Lock close to his own home – he had tried to slash his wrists and cut his throat, but in fact he drowned himself. Maybe he had heard someone refer to him as 'There's the fallen star'. But what a terrible irony lies in the Coroner's words: The verdict was – Suicide whilst of unsound mind'. Here was the man who had been retained at the old Pav in the nineties for four years whilst 'doubling' and 'trebling' the other halls of London; thousands had enjoyed his staccato singing style *à la* Mr Jingle, and his costume trademark of a long floppy coat and huge white collar.

Another earlier postscript to a painfully short life is about Nellie Power who died in 1887 at the age of 34. This postscript was acted out in the Clerkenwell County Court later that year before Mr Justice Eddis. A draper had sued Nellie's mother as executrix of the estate for £4.4.3d 'in respect of goods supplied to Nellie Power between February 1885 and June 1886'. Her cross-examination by Mr Popham, the plaintiff's solicitor, shows the straits her daughter was in:

> Nellie Power did not leave behind her an extensive wardrobe... Miss Power died perfectly penniless. She lived up to her means... She was on the boards on the Saturday before her death. It was at the Trocadero, but a very small engagement... Yes, Miss Power had costumes, of which witness took possession at the death... Certainly if she had five songs she would require five dresses... the dresses were very simple... The witness had the dresses now, value not more than three or four pounds... Deceased had no jewellery of her own when she died; the watch and two rings which she wore belonged to the witness... The funeral expenses were between thirty and forty pounds and these were not yet paid....

Mr Popham submitted that having proved the debts, and proved an estate, he should have costs. Mr Justice Eddis giving a verdict for the defendant commented: '... And there is not sufficient to pay the funeral expenses.'

One of Grandpa's songs expresses a performer's depression away from his beloved 'halls' and the cries from the audiences of 'Percy – Lost Chord... Lost Chord!'

> ... Everyone's too busy just to listen to my tunes.
> They hurry off, and seem to say 'Don't like it – join the loons!'.
> I struggle hard to strike a chord
> My wife gives me the bird.
> And yet to me it seems to be the sweetest ever heard.
> The Publishers have got my goat
> 'It's not commercial, dear old chap. I'm full of work. Good day.'
>
> But some day I shall get revenge
> When Peter at the Gate

Says 'Hurry Concertina Man, you've made it rather late'.
I've got the parts arranged by Jones.
The Golden Harps shall twang
'Concordia-like', those Heavenly tones
Shall go off with a bang.
A Halo they'll place round my head
A Toga just like Nero
As Music Scribe they will announce
Here comes — at last — a Hero . . .

On 24 September 1954 the Concertina Man finally 'made it' in his beloved garden at Cut Mill, Bosham, The last lines of his song could well have been his epitaph.

THE PRO'S LAMENT

. . . Seek a cosy combined
Furnished in old fashioned grace,
A picture of Randall, a po with no handle
And two ruptured ducks in a case —
Tha landlady's plump with two chins and a hump
And about her late husband she bleats.
She tells you with tears she's been letting for years
And you know that it's true by the sheets. . . .

That's part of the classic Rabelaisian *Pro's Lament* usually ascribed to Will Wise, a prolific writer for generations of comedians including Robey, Robb Wilton, George Jackley, Billy Bennett and Ted Ray. Hardly any of those old style Mas remain in this age of motorway travel — few pros today know how it used to be customary to put a live fly in your tea caddy to make sure Ma didn't 'borrow' any, or of the additional half-a-crown 'for cruet' added to the weekly bill of 15 shillings for self-catering!

There are dozens of 'landlady stories' but here's one of the rarer ones:
'Well, Gladys — I hope you didn't stand any nonsense from them theatricals.'
'Oh no Mrs Phelps — it has been a real pleasure. They're off to Scotland next.'
'Scotland? How d'you know that?'
'I heard the big one tell the little one they were going to scarper!'

The older generation of pros often used rhyming slang — a mixture of Cockney, Romany and Hindustani — and developed a private language so that Ma couldn't eavesdrop. For instance 'getting in on the wilkie' meant free admission on production of your professional card — 'wilkie' being short for Wilkie Bard, the comedian who died in 1944. 'Snow in the aris' was a pierrot saying — the 'aris' or 'aristotle' was rhyming slang for the 'bottle' or collecting box and 'snow' was paper money — a rare commodity in the 'aris'. Too often the waxi hommis would shout out 'Nanty Dinarly'. When in 1955 I was with the Douglas Head Entertainers in the Isle of Man, we always went round 'bottling'; a sure way of getting a good 'donation' was to interrupt a courting couple with an insistent 'Don't forget the happy pierrots!' and rattle the collecting box over them.

Douglas Head Entertainers
1955: top, George Boon,
Peter Honri, Harry Orchid;
right, two angles of Peter
Honri's solo act

In the same digs with me at Douglas was Tom McKay, an original 'Concordian'. He recalled working for Grandpa in the early days of *Concordia*: 'Certainly he was strict, but very fair. My brother and I got £8 a week joint, our fares paid and make-up supplied. Salaries were net, and there was none of the rehearsing for nanty with him. When we rehearsed, he always insisted that a proper lunch was laid on for all the cast − "Can't work on an empty stomach". He was one of the best.'

What is not generally realised is that today's pros lag behind the man-in-the-street, not only on salaries but on conditions in general − backstage conditions are usually inadequate, and sometimes quite primitive. The old timers seldom had a week out, work being so prolific, and even the smallest act made twice as much as the average wage-earner. Touring fares, digs and the other essentials of a performer, his band-parts, make-up, clothes, and baggage were cheaper. If he worked in evening dress, then a fifty bob 'off the peg' dinner suit crisply pressed before each performance could look like Savile Row on stage. Today's performer in the clubs knows that many of his audience have paid sixty or eighty pounds for their suits, but still expect him to outshine them.

Today's club decor presents an aura of glamour that is sadly seldom carried backstage, as this apocryphal story shows:

> 'Where's the dressing room, mate?'
> 'Eh?'
> 'The dressing room for the entertainers?'
> 'Oh − third nail down the passage!'

Fortunately most clubs are not as primeval as this in their backstage arrangements, but as I said when representing Equity at the 'Theatre '68' conference at the Guildhall on 10 October 1968:

> ... The majority of actors are working in existing theatres − perhaps going back hundreds of years; and the backstage conditions in some of those theatres, even in 1968, could be comparable with the theatre conditions perhaps at the Globe in Stratford-on-Avon and to any of the really early theatres. Some years ago [1961] Equity did a survey of the backstage conditions of 154 different theatres where members were working, and out of that 154 there were only 13 theatres where the backstage conditions could be compared with the average factory, or had conditions that would be suitable for somebody working in any other line of business than the theatre. ...

Backstage conditions and dressing rooms − these were things that Grandpa always used to get angry about, for as he said: 'A good part of one's life was spent backstage, and the better it was, then the better the show.' My aunt Mary has some 'fond' memories too of dressing rooms; as she related in a broadcast in 1963:

> ... Before the war, there were relatively few theatres that had good facilities. Perhaps the Star room would be reasonably comfortable, but the smaller one's name on the bill, the less one had to look forward to. The usual

room consisted of a long shelf as the dressing table with a mirror over, and maybe a light over it; otherwise it was an ordinary ceiling light of low wattage. Possibly some elderly lino on the floor, or a scrap of stage carpet that had finally proved too elderly for its intended use, plus one, two or three bentwood chairs according to how many were assigned to the room. Along one wall would be a batten with some hooks for the clothes to be hung on. The colour scheme was usually that horrid dark green or reddy colour half-way, with a lighter top. There was a basin with hot and cold taps, but that did not mean that there was any hot water. I've played in theatres where the water was brought round in a jug, and there was a pail to receive the dirty water, for the water was not laid on in the rooms.

It was no wonder that in those days of booming Variety with all the theatres open, most artists carried around with them the means of making their life a little more comfortable. We used to have curtains and covers for the dressing table, cushions and a rug, photos, vases of flowers; and our own cups and saucers and a spirit stove to make fresh tea or coffee. We had long dust sheets of the same material as the curtains with tapes all along the top to hang on the hooks and a return piece that covered our clothes when they were hung. . . .

Those 'dressing room soft furnishings' were useful in other ways too. Back in his single act days, Grandpa had gone with Malcolm Scott to do a charity appearance before their turns that night at the Holborn Empire. Malcolm Scott was a well-known 'dame' comedian, and after they had been dropped outside the stage door in time for 'First House', the cabbie drove off with his elaborate gown still on board. Malcolm had no spare costume at the theatre; but Percy Honri had an idea. . . . Nan was in the audience that night, and when Malcolm Scott made his entrance she thought his 'dress' looked familiar. It was. All Percy's 'soft furnishings' had been pinned, tucked and tacked together. The taxi driver brought back the missing gown, and 'Second House' never saw Percy's creation.

FIRST BRITISH DISC

'How the hell can I be funny into a funnel?' – that was Dan Leno's reaction to making a record when confronted with the recording horn. The whole paraphernalia of recording, whether it is for discs, television or films, even now can drain away humour. Technical advances with the development of the long-playing record and so on have made it possible to produce anything. Gone for ever are the limitations imposed by the two or four minute cylinder and the 78 r.p.m. disc. But even if the results were primitive and the comedy routines stilted, we must be grateful that so many of the music hall performers 'went on wax' and on to celluloid. A few have been re-issued on L.P.s, but most are still to be found hidden in the grooves of that highly breakable shellac. The labels on these records run into hundreds, as millions were stamped out and sold all over the world; recordings were pirated and performers switched from company to company. Naturally singers were recorded most, and Brian Rust has listed 453 Florrie Forde records 'and the sources by no means exhausted yet'. Les Kaye tells me he has over a hundred different recordings of G. H. Elliott, whilst another collector, Ernie Bayly, reports that Billy Williams, 'the man in the velvet suit' who died on 13 March 1915 at the age of thirty-seven, made over a hundred and twenty recordings on twenty different labels.

Born in Melbourne, Billy's first job in London was as assistant manager of the Marylebone Music Hall in 1901. It was here that he made his debut as a chorus singer. 'The man in the velvet suit' was his publicity gimmick, and he spent hours on the trams with his blue velvet suit and 'Bubbles' hair style, and soon became the talk of the town. An astute business man, be capitalised swiftly on his successful recording debut for Edison with *John, go and put your trousers on*. This exclusive three-year contract set down a flat fee of 50 shillings per recording, but he was able to prove this was only legally binding for cylinders and could not apply to recording discs. His popularity rose astonishingly, and he became a best-seller with his discs.

Labels Billy Williams recorded for included Pathe, John Bull, Homochord, National, Phoenix, Favorite, Cinch and Colisseum. One of the great favourites with the recording companies was George Formby Senior; he recorded for Sterling and Edison cylinders, and for Jumbo, Ariel, Odeon, Scala and Colisseum. His gentle style comes over clearly, and is comparable to the distinct diction of Billy Williams.

Grandpa's involvement in the world of discs went back to a date earlier than Leno's encounter with the funnel. On the 5 December 1946, Christopher Stone of the B.B.C. wrote him this letter:

> Dear Percy Honri,
>
> I met Fred Gaisberg today & was talking to him about the first disc record made in this country and he confirmed that it was a concertina solo with or without piano (himself or Eroli Dix?) in the autumn of 1898 but couldn't remember what titles you played. Not surprising. But can *you* remember? Have you a copy of the record in your archives?
>
> Yours sincerely,
> Christopher Stone.

Later that month, Christopher Stone wrote an article for the *Daily Mail*, and called it 'Jam Session 1897', although Brian Rust, the discographer, confirmed to me that the first 'session' was on 1 October 1898. This is how Christopher Stone set the scene:

> ... Percy Honri.... was a young man who played the concertina. One day he happened to be with Freddie Gaisberg – lately arrived from the Berliner outfit in USA and starting operations by making a studio out of a first floor room in the Maid's Head Hotel in Maiden Lane.... That morning a new Bechstein piano had been installed, and the German operator was busy with the recording apparatus that he had just brought over from Germany. Fred tried the piano, and Percy improvised on his concertina, and presently they had evolved the melodies and a brilliant accompaniment which they decided to record....

Above, still of Percy Honri in *The Schooner Gang* 1936; right, *Era* publicity cartoon; below, 'The Joking Windjammer' 1911

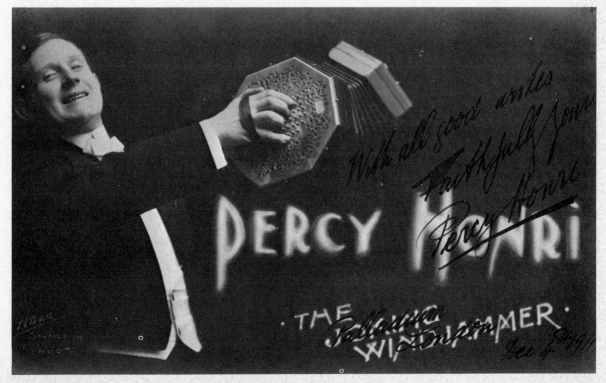

The title scratched into the shellac stamped with the E. Berliner trademark is '"Happy Darkies" Concertina P. Honri E. 9107 1.10.98'. On 3 October, he recorded *Austrian hymn*, and on the last day of October a two-part selection from *The Geisha* and an original composition *Coons delight*. I have a copy of this record, and even on the primitive recording the dexterity of his playing of the duet concertina is phenomenal − it is a kind of 'chicken reel', and must have formed a part of the act he was taking to America, because on 14 November he opened at Keith's Union Square Theatre in New York. I feel certain it was chance that enabled Percy Honri to make the first British disc. Freddie knew Percy was interested in anything new, and so the 'improvisation' became a recording landmark.

A postscript to those pioneer efforts occurred on Friday 21 January 1949. In a letter to me, Grandpa wrote: '. . . We were in London yesterday at the H.M.V. Studios re-making the No. 1 disc with the man that originally played the accompaniment for that historic record. Christopher Stone and most of the Directors were there, and we had a luncheon party afterwards. Quite good.' The recordings made at this unique re-creation are being released for the first time on the disc issued with this book.

Because of his touring commitments Grandpa made relatively few records of his concertina playing compared with his contemporary, Alexander Prince, who recorded prolifically both on cylinder and on disc.

PERCY HONRI − A DISCOGRAPHY

Happy Darkies	(1 Oct. 1898)	Berliner E-9107
Austrian Hymn	(3 Oct. 1898)	E-9113
Coons Delight	(31 Oct. 1898)	E-9116
The Geisha (2 parts)	(31 Oct. 1898)	E-9121/2

Recorded at the Berliner Studio, Maiden Lane, W.C., with Fred Gaisberg (piano).

In 1904 he recorded at Edison Bell Studios, Glengall Road, Peckham, a 'Two Minute' Gold moulded cylinder record: Concertina Sketch EB-964.

In 1910 he recorded for Nicole (D-128): Entry of the Gladiators, and a song and story from his act.

In November 1913 six titles were recorded for the Edison Bell Winner label:

3838−1	Oh You Silvery Bells	EBW 2501
3840−3	Tickled to death	EBW 2501
3842−2	Rubinstein's Melody in F	EBW 2542
3843−2	Barcarolle (Tales of Hoffman)	EBW 2542
	Miss Mexico	EBW 2569
	In the Sun − Intermezzo	EBW 2569

On Regal 1117, billed as the Laughing Loonies, Percy appears without his concertina with Fred Hearne, Charles Jolly and Kaye Connor in an 'I say − I say' type comedy sketch set in an asylum. Following their astonishing success in South Africa

on three visits between 1936 and 1938, Percy and Mary Honri made two recordings in Afrikaans for Columbia:

DE 111   Danie Louw   (CEA 2129)
          Ons dans so lekker   (CEA 2130)

Later in his career, Percy pops up on recordings made by friends like Charlie
Penrose – 'The Laughing Policeman', a character for which his wife Billie used to
write the script and lyrics. My Aunt Mary recalls that she and Grandma joined
Percy and Charlie on several records in the 1930s: 'There was one recording made
for India, for which Father brought out a very old concertina that had been stored
away and was rather out of tune – and how all of us joined in for the laughter. . . .'
Both Grandpa and Charlie were great collectors of antiques, and particularly were
they rivals in collecting Toby jugs. Here is the song Grandpa wrote about the
Toby jug for a film in which he sang a number of his own songs with Mary and
Vesta Victoria. The film, made in 1936, was *The Schooner Gang* – and Aunt Mary
tells me they were never paid for it!

Now all you collectors of china and such
That's been made by Frenchmen, by Germans and Dutch,
Give a thought to that jolly old boy Toby by name
Manufactured in Staffordshire by potters of fame.

There's an old Toby jug on the top kitchen shelf.
There's a smile of contentment on the old man himself.
When he thinks of all the jugs of ale
    that he has carried from the village pub,
No wonder there's a smile on the old Toby jug?

PERCY HONRI BOHEMIA

A MAGNIFICENT AND COLOSSAL COMBINATION.

An Entirely New Musical Phantasy, Invented, Composed,
Written and Produced by PERCY HONRI.

40 OVER FORTY TALENTED PERFORMERS **40**

Nine Magnificent Spectacular Scenes

Scene 1	-	-	EXTERIOR OF THE MANSION
The Hunting Party with a Pack of Real Fox Hounds			
Scene 2	-	-	INTERIOR OF THE MANSION
"The Dream"			
Scene 3			THE LAND OF BOHEMIA
Introducing Alexander's Rag-Time Brass Band			
Scene 4	-	-	AT THE STAGE DOOR
A Bustling Bust-up			
Scene 5			MEPHISTOPHELES' RECEPTION
Real Hot Stuff			
Scene 6	-		AN ITALIAN GARDEN
The Rendezvous of Music and Dance			
Scene 7			ON THE ROAD TO ZAG-A-ZIG
An Eastern Episode			
Scene 8	-		INSIDE THE BAZAAR
Gorgeous Tableaux of Eastern Beauties			
Scene 9	-	-	INTERIOR OF THE MANSION
"The Awakening"			

OXFORD MUSIC HALL
PERCY HONRI
EVERY EVENING

"CONCORDIA"

7   WE SING 'EM ALL

THE *Daily Sketch* photo bore the caption 'Caroline Emma Honri is a Blitz baby . . . but she is only five days old'. Yet the newspaper's date is 9 April 1962. That caption might have more accurately said 'the first Blitz baby', because Caroline was born whilst I was doing the dress rehearsal for Lionel Bart's musical *Blitz!*

On 13 April *Blitz!* opened a pre-West End run at the Regal, Edmonton—a great barn of a cinema, with a stage large enough and strong enough to take Sean Kenny's astonishing set. On 8 May we opened at the Adelphi, and for 568 performances I was a Battle of Britain fighter pilot escorting Toni Palmer down Petticoat Lane, as well as a busker on Bank tube station playing *Who's this geezer, Hitler?* on the squeeze-box. With *Oliver!*, *Blitz!* and later *Maggie May*, Lionel Bart emerged as the the dominant figure in the gutsy-style musical world of the sixties. His success stemmed from an idiom close to that of the music hall, but allied with the imaginative designs of Sean Kenny. The *Financial Times* critic T. C. Worsley observed: 'All the good old well-tried elements of the spectacular theatre of the nineties are worked in here . . . and Mr Bart, as sharp a showman as any in the business, knows that that's what the public will want. And they do. They always have done. Spectacle on the largest scale.

The Times described the set as being made up

> . . . of four immense mobile units representing the streets of the East End. With every brick face standing out a good three inches, these have an appearance of solid reality, and one of the magic pleasures of the production is to observe them moving into ever new formations. In addition to these there is a huge platform, the full length of the stage, which in the opening scene soars up to the flies disclosing an Underground station in which the cast are bedding themselves down during an air raid. With the aid of this marvellous piece of theatrical engineering and virtuoso lighting from Mr Richard Pilbrow, the production launches into ferociously lifelike replicas of the bombing. Fires burst out in back-projection; masonry crashes across the luridly darkened

Left *Blitz* 1962: 'Down the Lane' – photo. Barry Busbridge; below 1940 *Co-Optimists*, Arthur Ferrier's *News of the World* cartoon

stage, and lighting from the wings picks out the monstrously attenuated slum dwellings with their concrete steps and iron balustrades. The effect this has on the rest of the production is to lift it, on occasions, almost to the plane of epic. . . .

This was an extraordinary subject for a musical, and much of the success was due to the sincerity and sheer stamina of Amelia Bayntun, the mother figure at the centre of the story. It was an uncanny show to be in, if you had lived through the blitz. In 1940, we lived in a top-floor flat in Twickenham close to the Thames, and our 'shelter' was under the stairs — on bad nights in our neighbour's basement flat. But blitz or no blitz, shows went on if it was at all possible. It was around this time, November 1940, that a few lines in *The Times* announced: '*The Co-optimists of 1940* opens today at the Prince's Theatre, Bristol. Mr George Gee is the principal comedian, and the cast includes Mr Lyle Evans, Miss Phyllis Stanley, Miss Mary Honri, Mr Eddie Lattimer, Mr Ord Hamilton and Mr Ian Grant who has written the lyrics. The company is under the leadership of Miss Polly Ward. . . .' Remembering the show, Eddie Lattimer told me: 'Our next date after Bristol was the King's at Glasgow. When we got there we heard that Bristol had been blitzed and the Prince's Theatre bombed. A few weeks later I was called up.'

LEG-MANIACS ABROAD

Eddie's parents were both music hall artistes. A Broadhead programme, 11 September 1905, bills his father as:

Chas. Melton, Character Vocalist.
In an Original Military Song-Scena in two Tableaux entitled:
"The Reservist"
A true story of Everyday Life.

For a 1905 bill at the Brighton Alhambra topped by George Robey – 'The Monarch of Mirth' and also including Pat Rafferty; Clifton and Gibson – 'Comedians and Patterers'; The Labakans – 'Acrobatic Grotesques with their Wonderful Dog "Folly"; Walter King – 'The Sighing Comedian'; Lily Foy – 'Singer of Catchy Chorus Songs' and the Woellhafs (Fred and Marie) – 'The Versatile Pair', Charles Melton was engaged at a salary of £75 for the week by J. L. Graydon. His Brighton billmatter indicates that his sketch *The Reservist* was augmented by '. . . A Bevy of Beautiful Lady Lancers. Supported by Eight Elegant Cavalry Girls. The Cherrypickers & Numerous Auxiliaries.' The money, however, was better then the £17 per week John Coveney had paid for the act the previous week at the Royal Cambridge at Bishopgate.

Before her marriage, Eddie's mother Beattie was one of the 'Eight Cavalry Girls', and their double act was known as The Meltons, Charles Dare and Beattie Melton and later as King and Gold – 'Dutch Comedy Artistes, Wooden Shoe Dancers, and English Pedestal Clog Dancing Experts'. The pedestal top was made from a solid piece of slate in order to accentuate the beats of their clogs. Their

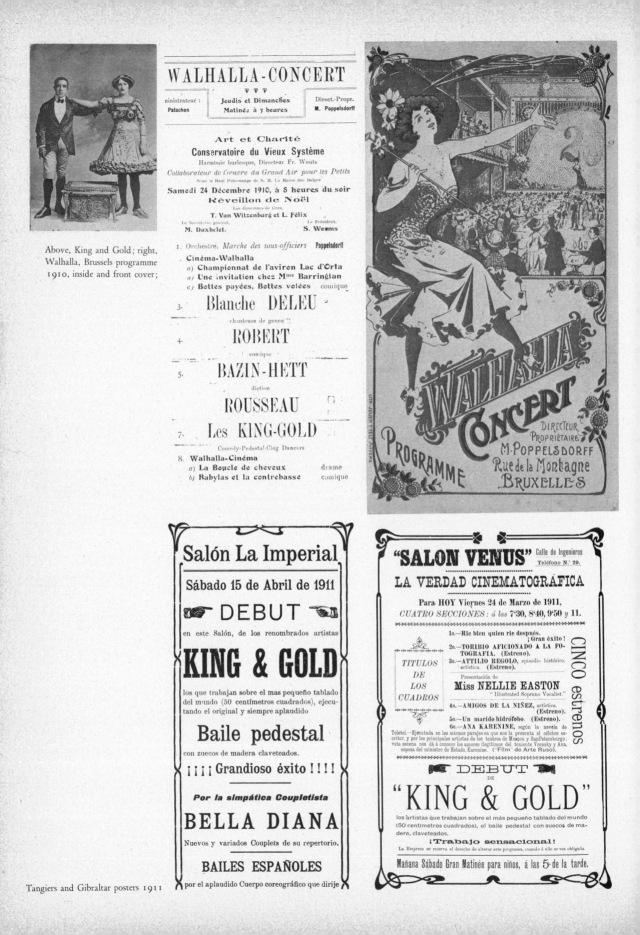

Above, King and Gold; right, Walhalla, Brussels programme 1910, inside and front cover;

WALHALLA-CONCERT

ininistrateur : | Jeudis et Dimanches | Direct.-Propr.
Patachon | Matinée à 3 heures | M. Poppelsdorff

Art et Charité
Conservatoire du Vieux Système
Harmbnie burlesque, Directeur Fr. Wouts
Collaborateur de l'œuvre du Grand Air pour les Petits
Sous le Haut Patronage de S. M. La Reine des Belges
Samedi 24 Décembre 1910, à 8 heures du soir
Réveillon de Noël
Les directeurs de fêtes,
T. Van Witzenburg et L. Félix
Le Secrétaire général, | Le Président,
M. Daxbelet. | S. Worms

1. Orchestre. Marche des sous-officiers Poppelsdorff
. Cinéma-Walhalla
   a) Championnat de l'aviron Lac d'Orta
   b) Une invitation chez Mme Barrington
   c) Bottes payées, Bottes volées comique
3. Blanche DELEU
chanteuse de genre
4. ROBERT
comique
5. BAZIN-HETT
diction
ROUSSEAU
7. Les KING-GOLD
Comedy-Pedestal-Clog Dancers
8. Walhalla-Cinéma
   a) La Boucle de cheveux drame
   b) Babylas et la contrebasse comique

WALHALLA CONCERT
DIRECTEUR PROPRIÉTAIRE
M. POPPELSDORFF
Rue de la Montagne
BRUXELLES
PROGRAMME

Salón La Imperial
Sábado 15 de Abril de 1911
☞ DEBUT ☜
en este Salón, de los renombrados artistas
KING & GOLD
los que trabajan sobre el mas pequeño tablado del mundo (50 centímetros cuadrados), ejecutando el original y siempre aplaudido
Baile pedestal
con zuecos de madera claveteados.
¡¡¡¡ Grandioso éxito !!!!
Por la simpática Coupletista
BELLA DIANA
Nuevos y variados Couplets de su repertorio.
BAILES ESPAÑOLES
por el aplaudido Cuerpo coreográfico que dirige

"SALON VENUS" Calle de Ingenieros Teléfono N.º 29.
LA VERDAD CINEMATOGRÁFICA
Para HOY Viernes 24 de Marzo de 1911,
CUATRO SECCIONES : á las 7'30, 8'40, 9'50 y 11.

TITULOS DE LOS CUADROS

1o.—Rie bien quien rie despúes.
¡Gran éxito!
2o.—TORIBIO AFICIONADO A LA FO-
TOGRAFIA. (Estreno).
3o.—ATTILIO REGOLO, episodio histórico,
artística. (Estreno).
Presentación de
Miss NELLIE EASTON
"Illustrated Soprano Vocalist."
4o.—AMIGOS DE LA NIÑEZ, artística.
(Estreno).
5o.—Un marido hidrófobo. (Estreno).
6o.—ANA KARENINE, según la novela de
Tolstoi.—Ejecutada en los mismos parajes en que nos la presenta el célebre es-
critor, y por los principales artistas de los teatros de Moscou y SanPetersburgo:
esta escena nos dá á conocer los amores ilegítimos del teniente Vronsky y Ana,
esposa del ministro de Estado, Karenine. ("Film" de Arte Ruso).

CINCO estrenos

☞ DEBUT DE ☜
"KING & GOLD"
los artistas que trabajan sobre el más pequeño tablado del mundo (50 centímetros cuadrados), el baile pedestal con suecos de madera, claveteados.
¡Trabajo sensacional!
La Empresa se reserva el derecho de alterar este programa, cuando á ello se vea obligada.

Mañana Sábado Gran Matinée para niños, á las 5 de la tarde.

Tangiers and Gibraltar posters 1911

scrapbook yields much information on performers working overseas before World War I. For example there is the *Gibralter Chronicle* review of their turn at the Salon Venus on 27 March 1911:

> ... The little cinematograph and variety show in Engineer Lane was last night filled to its utmost capacity at nearly all the four houses. The great attraction appealing to English people is provided by 'King and Gold', the champion clog dancers. The couple are also excellent low comedians and their work is of no mean order. We advise our readers not to miss the opportunity of seeing them. ...

There are copies of Army 'daybills' for their visits to The Citadel, Cairo, as early as February 1907 and to various garrison theatres in Malta during July and August 1908, entertaining the Fourth Worcesters at Imtarfa Barracks, and the First Battalion, Inniskilling Fusiliers, at Verdala Barracks.

In this country, too, the service town music halls like Chatham, Portsmouth, Aldershot and Woolwich were always extremely popular with the Army and Navy who enjoyed seeing themselves guyed, their exploits embroidered and their traditions praised in song and comedy walk:

'A funny thing happened to me on my way from Blighty – a sergeant called me "Sir!".

'After I picked myself up – I found I'd signed on for the Royal Standbacks. That's the regiment with a secret weapon – a shell that goes over and comes back with prisoners.

'Went for my medical – you know – if you're warm, you're in. Doctor tested my eyes – "I want you to read those letters on that wall."

'I said "Which wall?"

'So he put some garlic under my nose – "When you smell that you're amongst the enemy – fight like hell!"

'Told him "I've got fallen arches" – "Where we're sending you there are no hills."

'They put me on sentry duty – in the darkness I heard a sound – "Who goes there?" A voice said "Chaplain". So I said "Pass Charlie – all's well!" But now lads, here's a brand new Blighty song – "Hold the candle mother, while I shave the chicken's lip".'

> 'River Somme, my River Somme,
> Where the Boche lies low,
> Happyland, where all the day
> Rum-jars come and go.
> Trench to trench attacks we make
> With a nice aplomb.
> How we pray that we shall stay
> On dear old River Somme.'

George Robey's self-portrait; Bruce Bairnsfather's Ole Bill; Hetty King in her dressing room, Theatre Royal, Brighton

OLD BILL

During a 1970 season of music hall I did for Ronnie Brandon and Dickie Pounds at Newquay, I received a letter from one of the Old Contemptibles, Mr William Bick, recalling many nights spent at the Woolwich Hippodrome:

> I am 75 years old, and saw your grandad many a time . . . the Liberace of 1910 . . . and he was Top of the Bill . . . George Robey too, whose voice you could hear up in the back of the gods or shelf, which cost me 3d in those days . . . Chirgwin used to amuse me with his 'Goodnight, on the top shelf, Ladies and Gentlemen' and sit with a tray between his knees – and with two clay pipes would tap out a tap dance . . . Joe O'Gorman who sang *It's a long way to Tipperary* years before 1914, and got ratty because no one would sing the song.
>
> I joined up in 1913, and we sang it at camp not knowing then it would become world-famous as a marching song.

It was really George Curnock's dispatch to the *Daily Mail* dated Boulogne, 15 August 1914, which gave the fillip that ensured the song's incredible success: '. . .I can see them again with their brown jolly faces full of laughter and hear them singing "It's a long way to Tipperary, It's a long way to go".' Curnock was the only correspondent to mention the song in his description of the B.E.F.'s arrival at Boulogne – and Feldman's, the music publishers, suddenly found their song was a best seller.

Mr Bick's letter continues:

> I had joined up in the Royal Horse Artillery; you did three months depot training before you were allowed to wear the uniform. . . . We had hardly any pockets because the uniform was so tight, so in our peak caps we had a box of matches to keep the peak up – between the peak and the matches we had a packet of Woodbines, so if nobody was looking we would take off our hats – take a fag out and matches – light the fag, put the fag and matches back with three movements. Tap the hat and there we were. Anyway the Hippodrome was packed with Artillery, when on came Vesta Tilley in OUR uniform, and she did all the business with the matches and fag – even to bending and easing the tight trousers – she brought the house down. . . .

Mr Bick characteristically signs himself – 'Old Bill of the Better 'Ole'.

The impact and precision of Vesta Tilley, the eye for every detail of Hetty King, the charm of Ella Shields – these three were all male impersonators and great favourites with the troops because each one had an individual quality. Vesta Tilley retired at the height of her fame after an astonishing finale night at the London Coliseum on 5 June 1920. Don Ross said, recalling that farewell performance: 'I shall never forget that night, that enthusiasm, the tremendous emotional impact of the great wave of affection, admiration and sadness that swept over the footlights to the little figure on the stage. Her act was punctuated by applause, by laughs, by shouts of affectionate greetings from members of the audience. . . .'

Hetty King – Performer, a remarkable documentary film made by David Robinson, remains to remind us of Hetty, how her economy of movement enhanced the directness of her appeal even in a two-dimensional form. John Russell Taylor reviewing the film said: '. . . Hetty King emerges, at 86, not as a sweet old lady, but as a tough and exigent professional, giving value for money and very conscious of the craft behind her art. . . .'

Hetty first worked with Grandpa at Bristol as early as 1898 and she and his other old friend of sixty years' standing, George Robey, were on Percy's last bill at Portsmouth in December 1951.

As an Equity Councillor I was proud to be able to propose her for Honorary Life Membership of Equity – the highest honour that the union can bestow on a member.

There is also surviving film of the third member of that trio of male impersonators – Ella Shields; but it cannot really do justice to her memory. She was always a lady with ideas and schemes, as this interview for *The Stage* 21 October 1948 makes clear:

> . . . 'Hyde Park is not what it used to be' sighed Miss Shields, 'and that well illustrates why there is little hope for the male impersonator in the music hall of tomorrow. Forty years ago Hyde Park was a show in itself. . . . There was a holiday atmosphere about it all. It was the setting for a song. . . . It was simple to supply them in Edwardian days, but now subjects and inspiration are no longer at hand. To be a male impersonator it is not enough for an actress to wear trousers and sing a series of chorus songs. She must have a song that offers scope for characterisation. . . .'

The song *Burlington Bertie from Bow* was written for her by her husband William Hargreaves, and is surely one of the classic songs of the halls.

No one has kept a score of the number of performers who died in World War I. No one kept a record of the variety concerts organised at factories, garrison theatres and hospitals. But the music hall industry was involved, and adapted speedily to the constantly repeated catchphrase of the hour: 'Are we down-hearted? – No! No!! NO!!!'

Because of the static nature of much of World War I, there was little official organisation of entertainment – the stars twinkled in their own theatres, and their visits to 'Somewhere-in-France' were behind-the-lines affairs, often in proper theatres. Nearer the front, the Tommies relied on their own concert parties like Will Burnes's *First Army Follies* of 1917 and *Chips*. Another Forces show was *Les Rouges et Noirs* later to become *Splinters*, whilst in Salonika, also in 1917, Percy Merriman formed 'The Roosters'.

Grandpa sold war bonds from the top of a tank outside Birmingham Town Hall,

Percy Honri entertains:
at St Dunstan's; at home;
for War Bonds
at Birmingham, 1918

played at St Dunstans, and gave many impromptu shows for the wounded at his own home, Cromwell Hall in East Finchley.

In London, music halls and theatres boomed — but more and more revue was now taking over from the turns. The tempo of life was changing: syncopation was a part of everyone's world and music halls had to be as new as tomorrow with every presentation. 'Tommy-on-leave' wanted above all else to see glamour — light and colour and girls. *If you were the only girl in the world*, as sung by George Robey and Violet Loraine, provided for those who were on a few hours' leave from the horrors of the trenches the escapism they sought.

> . . . and, when he's laughed and said his say,
> He shows, as he removes the mask
> A face that's anything but gay.

These few lines from a short poem by Thackeray epitomise the dilemma of the performer in the savage world of 1914–18 where brother artistes of the International Artistes Lodge of pre-war days now fought hand to hand in No Man's Land. Into this world, a thirteen year old girl writes to Percy Honri at the Portsmouth Hippodrome during the last week of March 1917 — I think her letter, in a very personal and touching way, expresses the hope that lived amongst the carnage:

> . . . I expect you will be surprised, and think me a rude little girl by writing to you, but I felt I must write and tell you how much I enjoyed your delightful performance which I had the pleasure of seeing on Monday. I think you were just fine. You see I have been staying with Auntie who lives at Portsmouth for three weeks and came home yesterday. I did so want to come and see you before I came home, so Auntie took my cousin Dorrie and I. . . . Aren't you going to have your beautiful revue any more? I have seen it very often and should never get tired of seeing it . . . it was even better than a pantomime. . . .
>
> I expect you wonder why I love you so much, you see I lost my only brother Eric in the war early last January 1916, he died of wounds, and as you are so much like him, that is why I love *you* so, he too saw your lovely revue twice and said he never enjoyed anything so much. . . . Well with every good wish, and hoping your delightful act will always meet with success. . . .

ANIMATED NEWSPAPERS

> . . . Why have revues become so popular? I think for the same reason that the public appreciate a bright topical paper. A review is practically an animated newspaper. Comedians provide the jokes, song and dance scenas furnish living cartoons of passing public fads and eccentricities, and good humoured fun, through the agency of clever impersonators, is poked at men and women in the public eye whose appearance and mannerisms are well known. . . . I might prophecy that in the near future the best revues will practically be stage editions of a weekly newspaper. By that I mean happenings of the moment will every week be the subject of skits, topical songs, or scenas, in much the

same way as news is served up in interesting fashion and elaborated by the
newsfilm. . . .

These were some of Grandpa's ideas on revue as published in an article for *Titbits*
in 1915. He goes on to describe how he first began to formulate these ideas when
he was working with his parents:

> . . .I had the idea for the revue for many years before I was bold enough to
> produce it on the stage. . . . Roughly my idea was that the Pantomime Dame
> after January should be turned into a type of woman who was in the public
> eye in February, such as a temperance reformer, charwoman or school teacher.
> The Christmas Baron was to step into the clothes of a cab-driver or coster,
> and the lady Dick Whittington or Cinderella could change her identity to that
> of a popular actress of the moment whose mannerisms could be humorously
> mimicked.
>
> In those days I used to talk over my schemes with the late Dan Leno, with
> whom I lodged in several provincial towns. Dan liked the idea, and we were
> discussing the all-year-round pantomime on one occasion when he hung up a
> piece of brown paper on the wall and cleverly sketched a skit on the panto-
> mime demon's cave. Each goblin bore the likeness of a famous politician,
> and they were jostling round a cauldron marked 'Popularity' in an endeavour
> to get into the light-rays which bore the word 'Votes'. . . .

In his revue *What about it?* Percy Honri departed from the fantasy of *Concordia*
and *Bohemia* into the age when a reviewer dubbed him the 'Bleriot of the Halls'.
It is apparent that he used the animated newspapers idea, as this 'write up' of the
revue's visit to the Holborn Empire indicates:

> . . .In the true revue, the topics of the day and the outstanding episodes of the
> time should be tellingly caricatured – parodied, made fun of. And under all,
> the chief characters are playing out a little story. How many of the English
> revues fulfil this condition? Very few, it would seem – and so there are very
> few revues in the strictest sense of the word. However *What about it?* is a
> notable exception, and for this reason alone it should be seen by everyone who
> desires to know what a real Continental revue is like. There is a coherent
> story, and the topics of the moment are very much to the fore; and yet the
> production goes with even more swing than the disconnected 'turn' revues.
>
> All this only shows that the thing can be done – when there is the right
> man at the head of affairs to act as director. And it is quite clear that Mr Percy
> Honri is as much a master of the revue as he is a master of that much mis-
> understood instrument, the concertina. . . .

His revues were constantly revised to suit individual towns which he mostly
booked direct, renting the theatre and taking over the entire bill and ensuring that
the show was publicised. Back in 1908, in a letter to Oswald Stoll, he had pointed

May Fair Theatre

Licensed by the Lord Chamberlain to Jimmy Wollheim
The Theatre at the May Fair Hotel, Stratton Street, W1

DONALD ALBERY and JACK WALLER LTD.
(For Calabash Productions Ltd)
by arrangement with the May Fair Theatre

present

| PETER | JOHN | BILL | PETER |
| BALDWIN | DRYDEN | HEPPER | HONRI |

in

BEYOND THE FRINGE

the revue by

| Alan | Peter | Jonathan | Dudley |
| Bennett | Cook | Miller | Moore |

Directed by David Phethean

Setting designed by John Wyckham

Originally conceived and produced for the Edinburgh Festival by John Bassett.

First performance: Wednesday 15th April 1964

High Curley Stompers 1951, a jazz band formed and led by
Peter Honri at the White Hart, Blackwater, photo Ron Francis;
programme 1966

out 'we live in a picture age as type is too tedious to wade through'. His pictorial posters were always of a high quality, and his press publicity and advertising was usually ingenious — he enjoyed marrying photos and line drawings, or making clay models to photograph as individual items in a press campaign. Percy Honri was ever the showman and never skimped on giving 'value for money', even if it turned out to be a week of 'poor returns'.

His revue ledger gives a full breakdown of a typical week's expenses and takings — Hippodrome, Woolwich: week ending 8 May 1915.

May 3rd Monday	£114. 5. 10	Song Books £7. 10. 0
May 4th Tuesday	£117. 13. 3	
May 5th Wednesday	£126. 6. 2	
May 6th Thursday	£131. 5. 0	
May 7th Friday	£109. 2. 5	
May 8th Saturday	£189. 15. 4	
	£788. 8. 0	
Less to House	170. 0. 0	
	£618. 8. 0	Share at 50%: £309. 4. 0
		£316. 14. 0

The theatre management had to pay for the supporting company that week a total of £90 (The Poluskis £40; Beth Tate £30; Jack Stocks £10 and Stowe Bros £10). Percy Honri was able to bank £114. 13. 8, after paying the show's expenses of £202. 0. 4 which included items like: 'Revue Salaries £95. 16. 6'; 'Insurance Stamps 10/9'; 'Laundry 12/10½' and 'Newspaper Adverts 7/6'.

Supporting companies varied from week to week, and as the revue was on shares, salaries paid to the other acts were checked carefully. The revue ledger tells us that between 1915 and the start of 1917, when Percy reverted to his single turn, these were some of the salaries paid to the supporting acts: Mark Sheridan £75; Clarice Mayne £65; Tom Clare and T. E. Dunville £50; Two Bobs £45; Maidie Scott £42. 10s; The Poluskis £40; Joe O'Gorman £18; Jack Lorrimer £17. 10s; My Fancy £15 and Cecil Lyle £10.

My own experience of revue was sharpened when I took over the role created by Alan Bennett in *Beyond the Fringe* during its long stay at the Mayfair Theatre. It ran for 1899 performances at both the Fortune and the Mayfair, and I was with the show for two stints. In September 1963, within a week of my closing in *Blitz!* at the Adelphi, my agent Beryl Seton had negotiated for me to understudy Robin Ray, who had succeeded Dudley Moore as the pianist of the four-handed show. It was my third West End engagement, counting the short-lived *Lute Song* at the Winter Garden when I carried a spear for Yul Brynner! This was the first time I had been an understudy, and I found there was probably more nervous energy consumed wondering 'am I on tonight?' than actually working to an audience.

My second stint with the show covered the last six months of the run, and the intimacy of the Mayfair was perfect for the 'direct' style of the humour. Despite the sophistication of the dialogue, many of the best laughs were from pure music hall gags and situations, and I believe this sustained the show as much as anything.

The company manager of *Beyond the Fringe* was Henry Thomas, a most experienced stage director who had been with the show from its astonishing opening night. I had met Henry when I became engaged to June during the run of *White Horse Inn on Ice* at the Empress Hall; he had been stage director on all the shows June did there. A dedicated theatre man of the old school, he was able to communicate some of those tricks of stagecraft to the various casts of the show that revitalised revue in the 1960s. Henry remembered Percy Honri's idea of revue, and agreed that *Fringe* would have suited him admirably.

HER NAME WAS MARY

Tentatively the first bills listed 'Percy Honri assisted by Mary Honri', but soon the halls up and down the country announced Percy and Mary Honri – 'A Concert-in-a-Turn'. A brilliant soprano and pianist, Mary introduced the piano accordion into the double act; in a 1939 'write up', the *Daily Telegraph* said: 'Percy & Mary Honri present one of the best turns in this week's bill at the Coliseum, and one of the best musical acts in variety today. There is charm and artistry in all they do. . . .' Three weeks before the war breaks out, they are topping at Liverpool Pavilion: '. . . Percy Honri who is one of the few artistes on the stage today able to make the members of an audience, even a critical Liverpool audience, sing a chorus without first having almost to beg them to, is appearing with his daughter Mary. . . . They make an excellent team, providing both contrast and harmony in their playing and singing, and they were received with enthusiasm and an encore.'

September 3 1939 – Great Britain and her Empire beyond the seas is at war with Hitler's Germany. Again the performers do their bit, square bashing, spud peeling and making people laugh and forget for a while. Music hall relies more on the 'Radio Names' to top the bill, and some of these come a cropper in the flesh. Again there are the 'canteen concerts', the hospital shows, the 'Spitfire Fund' appeals, 'Wings for Victory', 'Dig for Victory' – the men from the Ministry have a slogan for every occasion. The infant television's bawling from the 'Ally Pally' has been silenced for the duration, but the inventive use of radio as a medium with its power to exercise the imagination is fast reaching its apogee. Everyone listening to 'Claude and Cecil' on I.T.M.A. put his own faces to them – just as almost a generation later Spike Milligan's Goons could be 'exclusive to everyone'.

In July 1944, I spent part of my school holidays 'on tour' with Percy and Mary Honri – we visited Morecambe, Rhyl and Oxford. I shall always remember one musical gag that Grandpa pulled before he introduced Mary: he played a cascade of chords and discords, and announced quietly: 'Hitler of yesterday.' Then the concertina hiccoughed a few random notes: 'Hitler of today.' He tagged the gag by letting the air out of the concertina's bellows with a mournful flourish: 'Hitler of tomorrow.' The audience loved it, and it always got a burst of applause. But, as the old pros say, 'it was tried and trusted'. Grandpa told me how in this way: 'I

Percy and Mary Honri 1937, photo. Howard Coster

Mary Honri 1935

BRISTOL HIPPODROME

TRAMWAYS CENTRE — — — St. Augustine's Parade

6.15 | **WEEK OF MONDAY, MAR. 11th, 1940** | **8.15**

THE MILLIONAIRE OF MELODIOUS MELODIES

"HUTCH"

(LESLIE A. HUTCHINSON)

IN NEW SONG SUCCESSES

THE VERSATILE COMEDIAN

G. S. MELVIN

FEATURING HIS LATEST AND FUNNIEST BURLESQUES

RADIO'S LAUGHTER MAKER

ROBB WILTON

IN HIS LATEST COMEDY OFFERING "A.F.S."

PERCY & MARY HONRI

"A CONCERT-IN-A-TURN"

HENDERSON TWINS

with DICK Jnr.   A SONG, A SMILE AND A DANCE

| LILY AVON DUO Sensational Aerialists | DON PHILIPPE & MARTA "Designed To Delight" | PIM'S NAVY The Bouncing Sailors |

ORCHESTRA STALLS	PARTERRE	GRAND TIER	BALCONY
2/6 & 1/9	1/3	1/6 & 1/3 Sats. & Hols. 1/9 & 1/6	6d. Sats. & Hols. 9d.

BOOK BY PHONE 21091 — BOX OFFICE OPEN 9.30 a.m. — 8.30 p.m

Percy and Mary Honri; top right, Robb Wilton, right, G. S. Melvin; Bristol Hippodrome 'day bill' 1940

used that gag in the '14–18 War, Peter, – the Kaiser of yesterday, today and tomorrow. And in the Boer War, when I dedicated it to Kruger!'

Soon Aunt Mary was 'on active service' herself. The *Chichester Observer* of 26 May 1945 devoted half a column to 'Miss Mary Honri, music hall artist, of Cut Mill, Bosham'. Mary had just returned home by air after eight months in France, Holland and Germany, and was soon off to entertain H.M. Forces in the Far East. The *Observer* went on to say:

> . . . She has been entertaining our troops with her singing and accordion playing, often right up behind the line, and was the first artist over the Rhine. She went with the first Ensa show to France, which included Nervo and Knox, Emlyn Williams, etc. They landed at Mulberry Harbour off the beaches in early September and had a great reception. She played with Ensa shows first, then was allowed to go forward on her own.
>
> Mary Honri played and sang in all sorts of places, from bombed out villages to orchards and hospitals. At Luneberg she played in the transit compound of the prisoners of war camp. She was bombed near Bremen and played on the Scheldt Islands.
>
> She has brought back an Army blanket with her on which she has sewn the insignias of some of the men she has entertained. She has sixteen dozen Corps and Division signs on it. Everywhere she met the same wonderful spirit among the men, whether in pain in hospital, tired out after battle, on the road, or just waiting around. . . . I asked Miss Honri which was our soldiers' favourite song. She said the three she was asked for most were *It's a Lovely Way to Spend an Evening, I'll Walk Alone* and *The Trolley Song*. . . . For the 50th Batt. Royal Tank Regiment CMF she sang their own special song, a parody of the ubiquitous *Lili Marlene*:

> Check your ammunition, T. and A. your gun,
> Synchronise your clutches so that she will run
> See that your wireless set's O.K.,
> Your mike will be DIS anyway;
> Then poor Marlene's boy-friend
> Will never get his way!
>
> If you meet a Panther, do your thinking fast
> Go like hell to flank him, hide your wireless mast,
> Your A.P. in back or side
> Will surely bust him open-wide;
> Then poor Marlene's boy-friend
> Will never get his way! . . .

MARY'S ENSA LOG

My Aunt Mary kept a diary of her Ensa exploits, and here are some excerpts in her own words to show another side of music hall:

... We left there early on 28 September 1944 in a convoy of lorries bound for Southampton Docks. It was a glorious morning and as we drove along we joined another convoy and there must have been at least 300 vehicles, and all the folks along the road waved to us, and were very surprised to see part of the soldiers were women.

Needless to say I found a soldier to give me a hand with my baggage. My accordion alone weighs something like 40 lbs and I had a case and zip-bag as well. We left about noon in the 'Louth' formerly on the Liverpool – Heysham run in peace time. In those early days though we sallied forth with a mass of equipment including solid fuel and a standard water purifier, 24 Hour rations, emergency rations, very hard tack biscuits, seasick bags etc. etc., they had completely forgotten about eating utensils and mugs! So you can just imagine the funny scene with all the Ensa crowd trying to eat a tinned steak and kidney pud served them on a plate only. . . .

After tea, Teddy Knox came looking for me to see if I would join in an impromptu show for the lads on board. I suppose there must have been 500 assorted troops on board, and not much comfort for them either. They had started to gather in the welldeck when I got there only to find that I was to be the concert! Still there were plenty of lads only too ready to sing, and Teddy Knox and Jimmy Nervo told stories. I think they would have sung all night but after it began to get rather dark, my pals from the top deck pushed their way through the crowd and carried me off to their mess for supper. . . .

In the morning I found we were lying some two or three miles off the famous Mulberry Harbour. Shortly after we had dropped anchor, a tank-landing barge came alongside, and all the troops and stores were loaded into her.

We landed on one of the smaller piers, and here we were a lot luckier than the soldiers as we had big army trucks to load up in, whereas they had to march. My first sight of battlefields made me feel quite sick inside. Some of the cross road villages were nothing but a heap of rubble, nothing could be distinguished, and everywhere the torn up fruit trees that produce the small apples for the famous wine named Calvados, after the district. . . . Our destination was St Aubin-sur-Mer. . . . There was an Ensa welfare officer who spoke French like a native, who had plenty of food laid on, including white bread and Camembert cheese – at just the right age. That meal of tea, bread, real Normandy butter, cheese and apples is one I shall never forget. The strangeness of the place, the different language, and above all the knowledge that we were at last 'Over Here', after our tedious waiting at home. . . .

When we were leaving home our Vicar had asked if I could possibly go and see his son's grave if I should be anywhere near Beny-sur-Mer. . . . The cemetery had been made in the corner of a field bordering on the little village, and was mainly Canadian. Apart from those tragic graves marked 'Unknown', I think John and his Bombardier were the only English there, but of

WELCOME TO YOU, MARY HONRI — OUR FIRST ENSA ARTISTE. ~·~

"AIRMEN'S MESS",
SOMEWHERE IN GERMANY
2ⁿᵈ MAY · 1945

Form E.B. 5

Nᵒ   3170

NO NAMES OF MILITARY UNITS OR OTHER FORMATIONS
SHOULD BE MENTIONED ON THIS FORM

DEPARTMENT OF NATIONAL SERVICE
ENTERTAINMENT

ENSA—INDIA COMMAND AND SEAC

| CATEGORY |
| AREA |
| ROUTE REF |

Completion Certificate

A Living Entertainment has been given by......*Mary Honri*..............

On (Day & Date)......*24*......day.....*October*.....194*5*

(Name of Party or Play)

** To { Royal Navy / ~~Army~~ / ~~R.A.F.~~ / U.S. Forces } *TENNESSEE* At *SINGAPORE*

Number Present.....*1500*........

Number of Performers.....*One*......

Times of Showing: { From.....*1900*.....To.....*2100*..... / From.............To............. }

NCO I/c..........................

Certified the above Entertainment was given *on the quarterdeck of the U.S.S. Tennessee upon her first visit to Singapore.*

(Signed) *L. V. Forde*

Lt. Cdr. U. S. Navy

Responsible Officer.

**Strike out services not entertained. In the case of mixed audiences give approximate percentages.

P (3) Y 99

Mary Honri's unique blanket of
badges, 1945; far left Airmen's
Mess poster, Germany 1945;
left, ENSA completion
certificate: USS *Tennessee*

Left, leaving for V-show tour (Mary at top)

Right and below, two typical forces cartoons from Mary Honri's collection

course, when I visited the place much later on there were many more.

Being the first Star show of the contingent to work, we set off with quite a crowd of people. We had very few props to take around, some shows had a mass of theatre baggage and always wanted to be there hours before the show – a thing I hate having to do; I like to get in just in time to get ready and go straight on. The theatre as we approached seemed to be an enormous tarpaulin covered place, which we were told had only been finally finished that afternoon, so you can guess our surprise when we went up on the stage and peeped through the curtains and saw rows and rows of beautiful new green plush and chromium-plated tip up seats! Apparently, the jerries had decided to have a theatre and our troops had captured this seating from some storehouse where it had arrived just before the attack. The theatre held 600 I think, but that night it was absolutely jammed, it was over a thousand more like, as the lads were like sardines.

On Sunday Emlyn Williams' party playing *Blithe Spirit* were to go to Bayeux, Richard Green's party playing *Arms and the Man* to Brussels. We were to go to Caen.

On Monday morning at Caen we went down by T.C. to see the theatre which was a shambles. It was amazing that the theatre had still survived. The main part of the place was all right, but the roof let the rain in and made such a noise that one couldn't hear a thing but the rattle and splash. Lighting for the theatres when there was no light in the town, was by generators. Halfway through our first show as the Mind-Reading act, The Kusharneys, was really getting going, the generator faded out. In the horrid hush that came for a moment, a very loud Cockney voice called out from the back of the hall: 'Now bloody well do it!' – and they did.

I had two spots of about 20 minutes, the first was me singing and talking, the second was community singing. However I was rather tired of the inevitable 'Daisy', 'Tipperary' and so on, so I had gradually evolved a series of songs from all over Britain and the Empire, and I sometimes did a bit of patter between each in the requisite dialect. I sing the chorus of 'Land of my Fathers' in Welsh, but here is the amazing thing, in practically every place as I started to play a Welshman would sing. Sometimes he'd stand up and sing, other times maybe there would be three or four together and they'd sing in harmony, with me joining in the chorus. . . .

Mary had hundreds of adventures doing her shows, especially being able to give a 'one-woman' show with her accordion wherever there was room to stand. One of the more unusual adventures was having a gun named after her. She told me:

Christmas eve afternoon 1944 found me standing in the wan winter sunshine reviewing number 4 gun's crew of the 420 Heavy Battery Royal Artillery, rather like visiting royalty. It happened thus. In September the Nervo & Knox Show had played a week in the little Church Hall in Nijmegen just after the Arnhem Battle with the Germans just the other side of the bridge across the Waal. I expressed a wish to pop off a gun at the other side just to show my feelings at having been separated from my husband Robert for so long — he was then with the Far Eastern Fleet. One of the officers said that he would arrange it. I was positioned beside the monster and told what would happen and what I had to do. The first round I would watch, and then come in on the second. I was warned to keep my mouth open as the gun went off. Before I could get my breath after the recoil, the ram had gone home, the new shell had been pushed in the breech, I was stepping across the sheerleg, the lanyard had been put in my hand and the officer yelled into my deafened ear PULL! And on Christmas Eve, having reviewed my gun, I gave another show and enjoyed a marvellous Christmas spread with the guncrews.

In September 1946, Mary was in one of the star-studded V-shows in Germany organised by the *News of the World* but this time the journey was made in a comfortably fitted out Skyways Dakota. Compered by Roy Rich and Brenda Bruce, the show included Sandy Powell & Co., Sirdani, Kenway and Young, Beryl Orde, Sara Gregory, Pat Kay and Betty Ankers and Cavan O'Connor.

There were many inquests into the role Ensa played in the war effort, and few were more critical than Paul Holt's in the *Daily Express* under the title 'Poor orphan Ensa — nobody loved her':

> ... The authorities will find much that is good in her, from the Hallé Orchestra, Sadler's Wells ballet, the great dance bands, down to a plump and jolly girl who spent the war wandering around front-line units by herself except for a squeeze-box. Her name is Mary Honri, the daughter of Percy Honri, the great variety star. The troops called her Mary. I think they never knew her other name. . . .

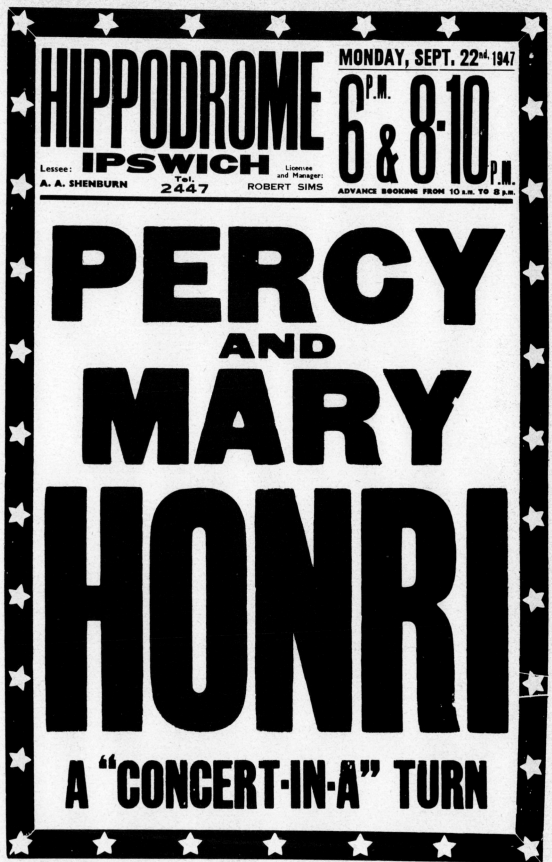

HIPPODROME

IPSWICH

Lessee: A. A. SHENBURN

Tel. 2447

Licensee and Manager: ROBERT SIMS

MONDAY, SEPT. 22nd, 1947

6 P.M. & 8-10 P.M.

ADVANCE BOOKING FROM 10 a.m. TO 8 p.m.

PERCY AND MARY HONRI

A "CONCERT-IN-A" TURN

1947 poster

W. E. Berry, Ltd., Nesfield Printing Works, Bradford.

8   WE ENJOY LIFE

ALTHOUGH it was the first of the London papers to accept Charles Morton's advertisements for the Canterbury in the 1860s, *The Times* is not usually a newspaper one would associate with music hall. But on 18 March 1932, it carried a three-column article on 'The Old Music Hall' by J. B. Booth, as one of a twenty-seven part series on the British way of life. There were fifteen illustrations, including photographs of the Old Empire in Leicester Square, the Oxford in Oxford Street, and of Charles Morton, 'Father of the Halls'. Other performers whose photos made that unique issue of *The Times* included Bessie Bellwood, 'a coster genius, whose "Wotcher Ria!" is still remembered'; Lottie Collins 'whose name will always be linked with "Ta-ra-ra Boom-de-ay"'; Vesta Tilley; Marie Lloyd 'noted for her breezy songs and quick Cockney wit'; Albert Chevalier; Arthur Roberts; Alfred Lester; Wilkie Bard; Dan Leno and Herbert Campbell, and a charmingly informal group made up of Leno, Coborn, the Bros Griffiths and their respective wives. As if this were not enough, the same issue devoted a leader to 'The Halls'. '. . . It was a natural world, an unself-conscious world . . . it was a world that did not see the need for any pretence. It did not pretend, because it was not afraid to be itself. It had its prejudices, its excesses, its stupidities, and its not unwholesome coarseness; but it was an honest, genial, and sturdily English world, which had not learned to apologise to the habitable globe for being English and for being its natural self. . . .' In his analysis of the 'variety' inherent in any music hall bill, the writer mentions the cross-talk men and trick cyclists, jugglers and tumblers, but stresses the impact made by the comic singers — men and women who 'had nothing but themselves, a song and a backcloth'.

Here is the synthesis of music hall. The nub of a performer's art lies in personality allied with the technique of 'selling it', of 'putting it over'. It is a chemistry that can be as electric as Shirley Bassey or as bland as Max Bygraves; as mischievous as Spike Milligan or as devious as Frankie Howerd; as eccentric as Max Wall or as friendly as Morecambe and Wise. Every one of these performers served his apprenticeship in the live theatre, and the other media have benefited from this experience. Television viewers may acclaim Bruce Forsyth, Larry Grayson, Ken Dodd and Petula Clark, but their expertise comes from live audiences, not from canned applause. As leisure became a fast growing industry, music hall was gradually swept away. Many managements, and indeed performers, believed the audiences would not desert them – but they lost them to other forms of entertainment. The only places where variety maintains a tenuous, sentimental foothold is the traditional Christmas pantomime and the seaside summer show at the large resorts – and even here it is the television personality who tops the bill. The new generation of variety performers will only find their regular live audiences in the clubs.

Clubland is not new. The clubs existed side by side with the smaller and larger music halls, but have thrived on an altogether brasher technique – the technique of the over-amplified mike, one-line jokes – a static yet free-wheeling art with the gold lamé jacket substituting for the 'cor blimey' gag.

Diverse and difficult to categorise, 'social clubs' have been booking artistes on a purely local basis for decades, the majority of them being part-timers. The 'social clubs' concert secretaries have formed federations to set up artiste exchanges, publish club magazines and lay down rules that performers have to accept without question, or they risk being banned from working any of that area's clubs. Sadly the concert secretary is often arrogant in his approach to an artiste and forgets his own union background of free negotiations.

Bearing a closer relationship to the music hall set-up are the proprietary clubs, the 'cabaret clubs' and 'dining clubs'. It is here that the pros have continued their touring days with their acts as known. Improvements in facilities have made also some 'social clubs' attractive to the pro and given him a further audience. His opportunities of a full datebook, however, are no longer there. His energies are concentrated more on getting work than on developing his presentation. The performer of today is constantly crying out for the chance to work – take away this chance and the law of diminishing returns will ultimately mean the end of music hall.

THE HANDSOMEST HALL IN TOWN

My belief is that the time is long overdue for the art of music hall to be officially recognised as part of the living arts by the Arts Council. Variety is accepted as popular entertainment but allowed to become self-indulgent and flaccid, to muddle along. Astonishingly, the theatre form that relates most closely to the people rarely achieves the critical acclaim and financial aid afforded to the other forms of theatre – music hall and circus are the skeletons in the British performing arts cupboard.

An opportunity to give flesh and blood to these skeletons is bound up with 'the handsomest hall in town'. This was how John Wilton modestly described his new music hall in 1859. What is remarkable is that this music hall still exists virtually as it was then. Ironically, it survived because in 1888 it became a Wesleyan

Top left, Marius Goring and
Lucie Mannheim in Noel
Coward's *Red peppers* Berlin
1959; above and left, Wilton's
Music Hall interiors 1972 and
1970, © *GLC Photograph
Library*

Val Elsey's artist's impressions
of a reborn Old Mahogany Bar
at Wilton's

Mission Hall, and in 1963, through the alertness of the British Music Hall Society and in particular its members John Betjeman, John Earl and Ellis Ashton, it became an 'ancient monument'.

The property had been included in the County of London (Grace's Alley, Stepney) Compulsory Purchase Order 1963, but at a public enquiry in September 1964 the Greater London Council gave an undertaking to consider the possibility of retaining the building. Later the Ministry of Housing and Local Government, in a letter of 15 November 1965, expressed the view that 'it is worthy of inclusion in the Statutory List of buildings of special architectural or historic interest'. At the moment (June 1973) the shell of Wilton's comes under the aegis of the Historic Buildings Board of the G.L.C., who are shortly seeking tenders for its lease. On 15 December 1972 a non-profit-distributing trust was set up, limited by guarantee and registerable as a charity, 'in order to raise funds to acquire the lease of Wilton's Music Hall and the property adjoining it, and to restore the Music Hall to its original purpose and to arrange for its use, and in connection therewith to do everything necessary which will assist these objects'. The five original trustees are Sir John Betjeman, Peter Cotes, Marius Goring, Don Ross and myself; the trust's patrons include Bernard Delfont, Sir Bernard Miles, C.B.E., John Osborne and Lord Olivier. A 'Roll of Interested Parties' was established immediately, and within six weeks over 300 people prominent in all walks of life had accepted our invitation to be entered on the Roll. Our parliamentary support already includes Baroness Lee, the Earl of Antrim, Andrew Faulds, M.P., Sir Harmar Nicholls, Bt, M.P., and Joan Quennell, M.P.

On 31 March 1973, Mrs Gladys Dimson presented the Greater London Council with a number of petitions signed by more than 500 Londoners supporting the trust's aims 'to preserve and re-open Wilton's Music Hall as a "National Theatre" of the Music Hall with Museum and Training School attached'.

As I see it, the concept of the trustees lies in allying the unique nature of Wilton's with a central music hall policy – with the peripheral assets of licensed catering, a museum and a school in music hall techniques. All of these are important to the public at large; and the scheme could mean that music hall performers would have their own 'National Theatre' and training centre. The Arts Council's 'Theatre Today' enquiry stated in January 1970: '. . . The theatre has demonstrated triumphantly that it has a national role and creative life of its own – a vitality which fertilizes an area far wider than its immediate minority audience', and that includes music hall.

During an interview with Georgina Walsh of the *Evening Standard* (25 January 1973), I rejected the idea that a restored Wilton's should be a museum of pub-based pastiche. I said: 'Music hall is an individualist art form. At its purest it is a caricature of reality. But it cannot exist in a vacuum, it has to ring true of today.' Within the existing Wilton's building there is space to salute the past, enjoy the present and nurture the future; and to provide the food and drink that is also a part of music

Top left, Jack Lorimer; top centre, Narow Brothers and Mlle
Lisette; top right, Daphne de Lisle; above left, Harry Lauder; above
centre, The Three Meers; right, Len Belmont and 'Charlie'

hall. My friend Val Elsey, F.R.I.B.A., shows in his sketches specially drawn for this book an impression of how John Wilton's original 'Old Mahogany Bar' could be refurbished and re-created. This bar was an outstanding feature of the Prince of Denmark public house when Wilton first took it over in 1850.

... WHO USE THEIR NATURAL VOICES TO ENTERTAIN

In accepting our invitation to become a patron of the Wilton's Music Hall Trust, Sir Laurence Olivier wrote:

> ... Can everybody possibly be enrolled in an anti-microphone faction?
>
> When I was preparing for *The Entertainer* many years ago, John Osborne took me round the outskirts of London to have a look at the last half dozen or so music halls remaining. And I saw as clearly as I have ever seen anything that it was the microphone that killed the Music Hall.
>
> The entertainer or the single act has a *weapon*, you see. No one can shout him down. He's protected by it, almost shielded by it and the whole spirit of gallantry and courage and temerity that was this medium's great attraction disappeared in front of your eyes.
>
> I remember noticing in support of this claim that if the diminutive figure, perhaps a female, ever danced away from the mike to one or the other side of the stage, the audience, which had been leaning back, flattened against the backs of their seats, started to go forward and when the 'artiste' returned to the centre – back they slumped again. . . .

The mike controversy will continue to rumble on; for whilst one obviously has to accept the necessity for its use in the mechanical media, it has become a sort of oxygen mask for live performances. My mother, Dorothy Wilkins, was a contemporary of Gielgud and Laughton at R.A.D.A. in the early twenties, and recalls the emphasis placed on diction. Prior to marrying Baynham Honri, she had worked both in the theatre and in a music hall sketch: 'We'd practise voice production reciting *The Times*'s third leader from the bottom of the garden.' Now what I call the 'music hall voice' does not rely on volume, but pitch and resonance – it is a voice with a cutting edge, and there are a few of them around still. A *Sunday Dispatch* paragraph (4 October 1953) recalls Grandpa's views:

> ... Throughout his long career he only once had to use a microphone to make his voice carry to the back of the audience. That was at a village flower show in Sussex, where he lived. Jet after jet roared overhead, disturbing his speech. Reluctantly Honri accepted the microphone that was offered to him. Into it he said sadly: 'The inventions of today mean the end of men like me who use their natural voices to entertain.'

VENTS

The ventriloquist forms an important aspect of music hall, and each era has had its own masters in the art. Many of the early performers used elaborate stage settings and a number of 'dolls' – Fred Russell's *Breach of Promise* sketch used eighteen puppets and dummies. Acting as counsel in a law court, he manipulated the figures by bulbs, tubes and wires. Another of the early ventriloquists, W.H. Clemart, also used up to a dozen heads along the top of a long screen. Both Russell and Clemart were pioneers of the V.A.F., and together with Joe O'Gorman and Wal Pink were known as the 'Big Four' — being in fact the first four on the V.A.F.'s roll of membership.

Fred Russell's 'Coster Joe', Tom Coram's 'Jerry Fisher', Arthur Prince's 'Jim', Johnson Clark's 'Hodge', Saveen's 'Daisy May', Peter Brough's 'Archie Andrews', Arthur Worsley's 'Charlie Brown', Dennis Spicer's 'James Green', Ray Alan's 'Lord Charles', Terry Hall's 'Lenny the Lion', Len Belmont's 'Charlie' — what a cavalcade of characters the ventriloquists have given us, their skills having invested each 'doll' with an individual life.

American ventriloquism's major influences were Edgar Bergen and the Great Lester. Bergen has yet to be topped as a showman, and was the pioneer 'radio vent' over twenty years ago with 'Charlie McCarthy' and 'Mortimer Snerd'. The Great Lester (Marion Czykowski) with his doll 'Frank Byron, Jr.' was a great originator in the art, and Walter Berlin, founder of the International Ventriloquists' Association, tells me: 'Lester is acknowledged in the profession as the greatest ventriloquist and vent teacher of all times. . . . He is credited with originating many of the common bits now in use by ventriloquists: the drinking and smoking stunts, the crying stunt, the 3-person phone conversation. . . .'

Other major American ventriloquial stars include Senor Wences, Paul Winchell, Jimmy Nelson, Clifford Guest, Shari Lewis, Dick Weston, Willie Tyler and Sammy King. Like their British counterparts, American vents have found niches for their brand of individualism not only in cabaret, but in trade shows and in educational fields.

When our music halls closed and work centred on the clubs, 'vents' adapted to the changed conditions, as Len Belmont told me: 'On the halls, the vents used scenery and props, but in cabaret they'd cut down the presentation to just puppets and a stool. . . . More novelty puppets came into use, and technique was much improved as they were working much closer to the audiences. . . .' Who can forget the sequence in the Ealing film *Dead of Night* where Michael Redgrave kills the dummy who has taken him over? So it was no surprise when Len told me that he was teaching vent techniques to a National Theatre actor for a Chekov play! It is the teaching of techniques like these that I envisage as part of the Wilton's Music Hall school training together with tumbling and 'timing', juggling and perhaps magic.

'A TOUCH OF THE VICTORIANAS'

In his play *A Touch of the Victorianas*, written for Thames Television's 'Armchair Theatre', Douglas Livingstone introduced a 'Victorians' concert party presenting 'Old Tyme Music Hall'.

Douglas Livingstone, like Osborne, Plater and Bennett, finds fascination in music hall lore. These playwrights appreciate the directness of the style, the constant affinity and sense of identification between audience and performer.

This computer uses magnetic tape to record information keyed in by the operator (top). The information appears simultaneously on a visual display (bottom).
Courtesy IBM Corporation

millionths of a second, or *microseconds*. The *third generation* of computers uses "monolithic circuits" that perform in billionths of a second, or *nanoseconds*.

The amazing speeds of the calculations done by computers are possible because electrons can flow faster than the hand can write. The progress from vacuum tubes to transistors to the newest integrated circuits was part of a trend toward miniaturization. Electronic impulses can be handled faster by computers with integrated circuits than by computers that have vacuum tubes.

The input placed into the computer goes to a processor, which is the central and most important part of the computer. This processor has a series of blinking lights that serve as signals to the operator about the calculations being performed.

A series of buttons also enables the operator to start or stop the processor as desired. An electric typewriter attached to the processor (or built into it) permits the operator to communicate with the processor and allows the processor to answer questions posed by the operator about material already in the machine.

The Arithmetic/Logic Unit. The processor has two primary functions. The first function is to perform the required arithmetic operations on the data fed into it and then store the totals. Thus its arithmetic section, known as the *adder,* may add, subtract, multiply, or divide as required. The adder can also compare the numbers to determine whether they are the same, lesser, or greater.

For their internal mathematical operations, computers use binary arithmetic rather than the decimal system, which would be used on an adding or calculating machine. The binary system uses only two digits, the "0" and the "1."

Binary arithmetic uses "bits" instead of "numbers." An example of one method of computing by binary arithmetic is as follows:

	Binary Value of Each Position			
Decimal Number	8	4	2	1
0 =	0	0	0	0
1 =	0	0	0	1
2 =	0	0	1	0
3 =	0	0	1	1
4 =	0	1	0	0
5 =	0	1	0	1
6 =	0	1	1	0
7 =	0	1	1	1
8 =	1	0	0	0
9 =	1	0	0	1

For tens, hundreds, and thousands, additional bit values can be added. To write 6,392 in binary-coded decimal form, the various segments would be written as shown below.

By using the binary system, the computer is able to add, subtract, multiply, and divide. The printed answers, however, are issued from the computer in decimal digits for ease of use and interpretation.

Main Storage or Memory. After the necessary binary computations are completed, answers are stored in the memory section that accumulates data. The second major function of the processor is to supply information from the internal memory of the system or to update the memory portion and hold it in readiness until it is needed again. Just as our brains store many items and recall them as needed, so the storage or memory section of computers will store information, such as data related to different charge accounts, and recall that information as needed at a later time. The internal memory of a computer is one of its most distinctive and valuable assets. Even if its computations were not lightning fast, its ability to store and retrieve material almost instantly while occupying minimal space makes it invaluable.

Output

All the valuable information processed and stored by the computer must be supplied in a form that can be used by the people who must make decisions based on the data. Computers therefore have some method of producing output that translates the binary computations that have been performed electronically into readable numbers (numeric output) and words (alphabetic

VALUE OF EACH POSITION

	Thousands				Hundreds				Tens				Units			
	8	4	2	1	8	4	2	1	8	4	2	1	8	4	2	1
6,000	0	1	1	0												
300					0	0	1	1								
90									1	0	0	1				
2													0	0	1	0
6,392	0	1	1	0	0	0	1	1	1	0	0	1	0	0	1	0

output) or words and numbers (alphanumeric output). Printers are amazingly fast. They can print hundreds of lines of numbers and almost as many lines of alphabetic and numeric material at great speed. Printed reports may be used for analysis by the managers of a firm. They may be the actual bills that will be sent to customers. Or they may contain information to be placed into the computer again for combination with other data. Some output operations use typewriterlike devices. These devices act like old-time player pianos—typing without anyone near to issue the report from the computer.

STEPS IN DATA PROCESSING

Whenever retailers receive an article from a vendor, whenever they sell a product to a customer, or whenever they pay their employees for the work they have performed, all the necessary information must go through certain processes. Data must be recorded, coded, sorted, computed, summarized, and communicated.

Recording

Information about goods or people must be listed or recorded in an efficient manner so it can be found easily and used effectively. The speed and accuracy of recording information are important for all the other steps in data processing. Data may be recorded on sales checks, on cash register tapes, on invoices, on employee time cards, or in ledgers or journals. Data may be recorded on more up-to-date devices such as punched tapes or punched cards or tags, or it may be recorded directly through terminals that are on-line to the computer. Data may have to be recorded several different times.

Coding

Retailers must code or label each kind of transaction before or after it has been recorded so that it can be properly identified. Thus all transactions having to do with products sold to customers would be coded one way, while those pertaining to paying the employees would be coded another

way. Transactions pertaining to a vendor's bills would be coded in still another way. Transactions might also involve supplies, rent, taxes, and cash receipts. Each type of transaction would be given an appropriate code, and then each major coding classification would be broken down into many subclassifications. For example, customer transactions would go under one code number. The merchant would want to know the nature of each customer transaction. Therefore, other code numbers would tell whether the transaction involved cash, a charge card, or a COD arrangement. The merchant might also want to know which customers were involved. Consequently, a code number or label would need to be assigned to each customer so that each could be identified when necessary. In this way, if a retailer wanted information on one customer's account, that retailer would be able to obtain the proper figures with ease. Coding is an enormous task because each person and each item of merchandise must be easily identified. The Universal Product Code is currently being used on prepackaged items. It is discussed later in this chapter.

Sorting

After transactions have been coded, they may be sorted according to code. All transactions relating to payrolls will be placed in one area; those pertaining to accounts payable (vendors' bills) will go to another area; those pertaining to accounts receivable (customers' charge accounts) will go to still another area. Further sorting will then be done within those various groups. If the initial coding is not properly done, however, the sorting cannot be accurate.

Computing

When the sorting of all the coded transactions has been done, the computing or necessary figuring can be performed. Payments to vendors, payments for rent, payments for taxes, and amounts due on charge accounts are figured. Payrolls may be computed weekly or monthly by multiplying the total hours each employee worked by the amount of money earned per hour. Assessments against each salary, such as income tax, social security payments, health plan dues, and union dues, are then deducted from the total.

Summarizing

Totals are calculated for each type of record. Each kind of payroll deduction, for example, would be recorded in a separate category so that the retailer would know, besides the total amount of deductions from each employee's pay, the total withheld for income taxes, for union or other agency dues, or for insurance or health plans. This summarizing organizes the different groups of facts and figures of the whole data collection into a usable form. Thus the managers can tell how money is being spent, and they can analyze expenditures group by group.

Communicating

Since data processing is used to accomplish the mathematical functions of a business, the data must be communicated to the accounting area where a final report of the assembled facts can be made.

PROGRAMMING THE COMPUTER

"Do computers think?" is a question often posed. A computer does not do anything on its own. It is a machine that performs only upon direction. Programmers are needed to tell the machine what to do and how to do it. Programmers need to know the problems of the business for which they are developing computer programs. They must have the skill to translate these problems into tiny segments, then into flowcharts, and finally into a form the machine can understand. Therefore, they must be highly specialized workers. Every firm that uses computers on its own premises must have one or more programmers on its staff.

Programmers perform two primary tasks in programming a computer. First, they must break down directions and give them step by step. Second, they must give directions in a language the machine can use and interpret. For business, the most commonly used language is COBOL (Common Business Oriented Language).

Since the machine can perform only as instructed, each program must be correct so that the output is correct. In referring to computer errors, a term commonly used is "GIGO" (pronounced guy-go), meaning "garbage in—garbage out." The machine processes incorrect as well as correct information. Therefore, special care must be taken to program it accurately. One slight miscalculation by a programmer in a Midwestern city caused 85,000 charge customers to receive incorrect bills. It took months to straighten out this error.

PROVIDING ELECTRONIC DATA PROCESSING FOR RETAILING

When a retailing operation has been successfully run on a manual recordkeeping system, some managers are reluctant to change to another system. However, as more retailers convert to electronic data processing (EDP), the competition they offer other retailers in their community is stepped up. The EDP-equipped retailer is able to speed reorders, reduce inventory and therefore reduce costs, quickly record customers' bills, update accounts payable records daily, and generally run a more efficient organization. This efficiency permits the retailer to handle more customers with ease. More and more retailers have to convert to EDP to enjoy this efficiency.

Various ways of obtaining the equipment, or hardware, are available to the retailer: buying, renting, or using service plans.

Purchasing Equipment

Large or multi-firm retailers who can make 24-hour-a-day use of computer equipment may buy the equipment they need. However, the high costs of equipment and the fact that newer models with greater speed and added storage and output abilities are frequently appearing have made buying undesirable for most retailers.

Renting Equipment

The high cost of renting equipment may be justified only if the equipment can be kept in almost constant use. Even though the retailer rents the equipment, the store must hire and train its own personnel to run the machines. Rental plans usually include service charges for "down time" repairs.

Using Service Plans

For smaller firms that cannot afford to purchase or rent the costly equipment, and for those firms that cannot keep the machines in constant use, service centers are available where material may be processed for a service charge. The service center provides the personnel needed to do the processing of the data, including the programming, and certain time periods are assigned for each firm being serviced. By this means, even small retailers who need detailed records may have computer recording available.

PROBLEMS OF CONVERSION TO ELECTRONIC DATA PROCESSING

When a retailing firm plans to convert from a manual system to a computer system for the various activities within the organization, a number of important steps must be taken.

- The firm must create a conversion calendar, which will serve to set the plans for the activities to take place. This must be adhered to as closely as possible.

- The firm must propose that major changes coincide with periods when the store personnel are not overburdened with routine store activities. Periods when business is slack are generally best for conversion.

- The firm must select a clerical staff that can work on both manual and, later, computer facilities.

- The firm must hold frequent meetings so that every person understands what is taking place. Those directly concerned should meet daily.

- All plans should be written out so that there can be no misunderstanding, no omission of any important detail, and no chance to forget the agreements made.

- The firm should carry out every planned activity. Forms must be ordered; step-by-step programs must be planned; personnel must be trained. Everything must be accomplished.

- The manual and computer systems should be tested simultaneously to make sure that everything is working correctly. The manual system has to be checked against the computer system and the computer system against the manual system to make sure that complete data are present and correct as the new system takes over.

THE IMPACT OF THE COMPUTER ON RETAILING

Electronic data processing has potentials for use wherever counting, computing, and recording must be done. Every division of retailing firms can make use of EDP. Accounts receivable, accounts payable, merchandising unit and dollar control, and payroll are all divisions that lend themselves to speedier and more accurate recordkeeping through EDP.

Supermarket Checkout Using the Universal Product Code

Some mass merchandisers and supermarkets across the country use the newest, speediest, most accurate method of registering supermarket merchandise sales available. Merchandise is premarked by manufacturers with a *Universal Product Code,* (UPC)—inked lines of different widths and lengths that represent numbers. These numbers tell all about the product: its size, weight, color or texture, and manufacturer, and what the item itself is. Only the price is not included in this code. The operator moves the coded merchandise across the surface of an optical scanner. Immediately the scanner reads the inked lines on the product and relays the facts to

```
        HOMETOWN FOOD MART
        STORE 123    04/20/7-


    GRO    .54F  CEREAL
    NFD   3.90H  WINSTON
    GRO    .57F  CHILI
    MT    1.13F  T BONE
    NFD    .43C  KLEENEX
    PRO    .47F  BANANA
    NFD    .19C  DOG FOOD
    NFD    .35C  GLAD WRAP
    GRO    .07F  KOOL AID
    GRO    .07F  KOOL AID
    GRO    .06F  KOOL AID

           .06   TAX

          7.84   TOTAL

         10.00   CASH

          2.16   CHANGE

    0007 02   4   4.22PM
```

As the optical scanner (top) reads the Universal Price Code (bottom left), the price is flashed on a screen and is recorded on an itemized sales slip (bottom right).
Courtesy NCR Corporation

the computer. The computer matches the price to the code. Prices may be changed as frequently as desired simply by putting new price information into the computer. As the code on each piece of merchandise is read by the scanner, the price is flashed on a screen for the customer to see, just as a cash register shows a price. At the conclusion of the sale, an itemized sales slip is issued from the machine for the merchandise purchased, and the cashier either rings up the customer's money and makes change or records the total against the customer's charge account. Through the use of the Universal Product Code and the fixed scanner (a movable wand scanner may also be used), customers move through the lines faster. This means that fewer cashiers and baggers are needed and the costs of doing business are reduced—resulting in lower prices for goods.

Integrated Data Processing

The ideal EDP system is the one in which data are captured at the *point of sale* from the price tag attached to the goods or from the Universal Product Code printed on the label. The data thus obtained are used repeatedly throughout the store's recordkeeping system. This is known as *integrated data processing.*

The information taken from the price tag or the UPC is either punched into the cash register terminal or scanned by a wand or a fixed scanner. The following information is retrieved and computed or recorded:

- The item, and its style number, size, and color
- The season letter of the item (representing the month or week it entered the store's stock)
- The manufacturer of the item
- The retail price of the item sold
- The department or area where the item was sold
- The identification of the salesperson who sold the item

- The tax on the item, if any
- The type of sale, such as cash take, cash send, charge take, charge send, or COD
- If a charge sale, the name and account number of the person to whom the merchandise is charged

The information about the merchandise sold will be sent automatically to the merchandising division, which will update the unit-control records to show that those particular items were sold. The merchandising division will refigure the totals to determine the number of articles of that style, color, and size, for example, that now remain on hand. When the number on hand reaches a preset low point, an order will automatically be printed for the vendor, and a new on-order total will be entered in the unit-control records for that merchandise. Simultaneously, other records will be adjusted to indicate what dollar amount remains in that period for purchases. Accounts payable records will be updated when the new merchandise arrives so that the store will know what it owes to the vendor.

Similarly, the records for the customer's account for charge sales will be updated. The records of the salesperson's sales will also be adjusted. If the salesperson sells on commission, the new amount owed to that person as a result of this sale will be computed.

EXCEPTION REPORTING

The computer, as you have learned, can supply large amounts of information rapidly. Thus, for example, if a firm wanted to update customers' charge accounts daily, the computer could do this. However, no person in the firm would be able to read the daily reports about some 20,000 or more customers. Nor would customers want to receive bills on a daily basis. Consequently, the large amounts of data that can be poured out of the computer need to be handled selectively. If a situation is unusual or needs the immediate attention of a manager, the necessary information should be available immediately. *Exception reporting* that selects only problem areas, critical items, or unusual activity at a given time, while holding ordinary reporting for periodic output, has proved to be immensely valuable to retailers.

For example, assume a customer's credit rating allowed charges on his or her account up to $300 per month. Suddenly this customer makes a large number of purchases in one day totaling over $300. The computer would print a report about this account alerting the store's manager to this sudden flurry of activity. The manager could then determine what action is necessary, or the computer would signal that further credit would not be granted.

For the unit control of merchandise, exception reporting is ideal. If, during a normal period, sales for an item were 24 units weekly, the machine could be programmed to issue no report for sales activity for the item if between 18 to 30 units were sold weekly. If, however, 31 or more units were sold during one week, or if fewer than 18 units were sold, the machine would issue a report to alert the buyer to the unusual situation occurring in the sales of this item. The buyer could then take the necessary action to ensure adequate stock for the department or to get rid of the surplus.

THE MANAGER'S ROLE IN HANDLING COMPUTERIZED POINT-OF-SALE RECORDS

While an integrated data processing system eliminates much of the tedious recordkeeping that used to be done by hand, it does not reduce the decision-making workload of the executives or the management team. The computer merely counts, stores data, tabulates, and does routine ordering. Making special decisions, selecting new merchandise, changing merchandise lines, determining which customers' accounts are poor or questionable risks, deciding which salespeople are doing the best job—these tasks and countless others continue to be the responsibility of the management team in retailing.

TOPICS FOR DISCUSSION

1. Why have retailers turned to electronic data processing for recordkeeping?
2. Explain briefly the steps necessary in processing data.
3. What is the advantage of the internal memory of a computer?
4. What is meant by the term "alphanumeric output"?
5. What is the role of a programmer?
6. Why do some retailing firms use EDP service plans instead of purchasing or renting EDP equipment?
7. Why should both manual and computer systems be maintained simultaneously during conversion to electronic data processing?
8. What two types of optical scanners are available?
9. Why is point-of-sale computer recording being used increasingly?
10. What is meant by "exception reporting"? Why is it used?

MATHEMATICS FOR RETAILING

On a separate sheet of paper, write the following numbers in the binary system:
(a) 374, (b) 55, (c) 8906.

Top, still from Thames
Television's *A touch of the
Victorianas*: Peter Glaze and
Peter Honri, *Courtesy Thames
Television*; left, Peter Honri as
'The immaculate hobo'

When one considers the hundreds of songs that were sung during the days when the chairman ruled the roost with his hammer, how unimaginative are most 'Old Time' shows, both amateur and professional, in their selection of material. *The Stage* (10 January 1901) carries an advert for Francis, Day and Hunter songs, and some of the titles look as if they are worth investigating instead of trotting out *My old Dutch* or *The Cock Linnet Song* of Marie Lloyd.

'Folkestone for the day' (Bateman & Le Brunn)	Sung by Marie Lloyd
'Feminine moods & tenses' (Harrington & Le Brunn)	Marie Lloyd
'Though her head is bent with age' (Barnes & Collins)	Kate Carney
'Becos she 'as a 'andle to her name' (Dalton & David)	Gus Elen
'My next door neighbour's garden' (Bateman & Le Brunn)	Gus Elen
'Drink: by a party who has had some' (Dickson & Randall)	Harry Randall
'The Boers have taken my Daddy' (Mills & Castling)	Tom Costello
''Ackney with the 'Ouses took away' (Bateman & Le Brunn)	Vesta Victoria
'I wouldn't lend you very much of that' (Bateman & Lee)	Herbert Campbell
'The war correspondent' (Chas. Osborne)	T. E. Dunville
'Oh Jack, you are a handy man!' (Nat Clifford)	Katie Lawrence

Most artistes used original songs, of which they had purchased sole performing rights for a pound or two. The successful songs were usually published, the writer splitting the royalties fifty-fifty with the performer, but the sheet music usually stated that the song could not be sung in a music hall. This copyright of songs was jealously guarded in those days, and woe betide any 'wines and spirits' who purloined a top of the bill's song and hoped he'd not be found out. But one star did lose her case against a theatre for using her copyright song. The star was Katie Lawrence and the song was *Daisy Bell*. In 1895, according to *The Era*'s 'Dramatic and Musical Law' published in 1898, Katie had 'sought to recover 312 penalties of 40/- each for the infringements of her right to the song from the Blackpool Winter Gardens and Pavilion'. In December 1892, before the song had been published or sung in public, Katie Lawrence purchased from Harry Dacre the sole right and liberty of performing the song in Great Britain. The report continues: '... When the song was subsequently published it bore upon the title page the

This Week....August 18th 1903

Next Week....

In Consideration of the sum of
One Guinea, I hereby assign to
Percy Honri the sole singing and
performing rights of the song written
and composed by me and entitled
"Conclusions". It being mutually
agreed that in the event of
publication I receive one half of
the proceeds Signed this
18th August 1903

Nat Mayer

Above, composer's assignment; top right, 1903 song cover; far right, *Era* cartoon; right, Eugene Stratton without burnt cork

following notice: "This song may be sung in public without fee or licence except at Music Halls".' *Daisy Bell* was sung in a pantomime, and Katie Lawrence sued the Winter Gardens, contending that the song was a 'dramatic piece' within the meaning of the Copyright Acts. On this *Daisy Bell* case, Lord Justice Smith of the Queen's Bench said: '. . . It is an entire misnomer to call a mere, common, ordinary music hall song, which requires neither acting nor scenery for its production, a dramatic piece, for it is nothing of the kind. In my judgement, as a matter of fact, this song *Daisy Bell* is not a dramatic piece; if it were every boy in the street who sung it would be liable to be proceeded against for having performed a dramatic piece without the written consent of the author, which is wholly untenable.' It would seem though that Lord Justice Smith's judgement on the song's worth is rather awry – *Daisy Bell* is perhaps the best-known music hall song of all.

Another famous music hall song is *At Trinity Church I met my Doom* which was originally sung by Will Turner in concert party, but it was made a success by Tom Costello who not only adopted it but also copied Will's gait stumping across the stage whilst singing. Apparently one of Will Turner's legs was shorter than the other. Grandpa told me of the time Tom Costello was due to meet him in the West End. Tom arrived late and, apologising profusely for his lateness, said 'The Band of the Grenadier Guards were playing *At Trinity Church* marching down White-hall, and when I heard all those trombones go pom pom pom pom, Percy, I had to march with them!'

Everyone knows the tune of *Lily of Laguna*; it was composed by Leslie Stuart and sung initially by Eugene Stratton. After Gene Stratton died in 1918, G. H. Elliott added it to his repertoire. The London Pavilion was a favourite hall of Stratton's and Grandpa was often on the same bill with him. One particular week, Gene was scheduled to present a new song by Leslie Stuart. The first night of a new song was always well advertised and for the setting and the band rehearsals the theatre was locked and only those directly concerned with the show were allowed in. Grandpa, who was also at the 'Pav' that week, managed to sneak in and hid himself where he could watch proceedings.

Later that evening he said to Gene that he thought he had a song that would interest him, and he played him the song that he had listened to at that private bandcall. Poor Gene was thunderstruck, and rightly so, for he was to sing it the next night, and did not dream that anyone could have got into the theatre whilst he was rehearsing. He demanded to know how Percy had picked on exactly the same melody, and he was all for phoning Leslie Stuart at once to put off the song. So Grandpa told him what he had done, and Gene roared with laughter at the leg-pull, and no doubt recounted it at the Water Rats lodge meeting. Grandpa himself composed over 250 songs. He would write about anything – even his own opera-tion in 1936 was a source of inspiration. Convalescing on a voyage to South Africa, where Aunt Mary was doing a pantomime season, he wrote:

Top, Water Rats dinner, including: Percy Honri, Whit Cunliffe, Carlton, Sammy Shields, Dave Carter, Bill Kellino, George Sanford, Egbert Brother, Alf Leonard, Seth Egbert, Hedges Brother, Harry Blake, R. Protti, Geo. Leyton, Morny Cash, Arthur Astor, Lupino Lane, Marriott Edgar, Harry Barratt, Egbert Brother, Geo. Mozart, Sam McCarthy, J. W. Cragg, Lew Lake, Joe O'Gorman, Joe Elvin, Fred Russell, Harry Tate, Harry Weldon, Jack Lotto; 1936 Water Rats cartoon by Seth Egbert

Thanks for the Memory company: right, Randolph Sutton, Nellie Wallace, G. H. Elliott, Gertie Gitana, Billy Danvers, Ella Shields, Talbot O'Farrell; below, Nellie Wallace, Gertie Gitana, Mrs. G. H. Elliott, Don Ross, G. H. Elliott, Ella Shields 1948

Oncest on a time I felt real proper bad,
So I went down to t'Doctors an' 'e says 'Eh; Lad.
It's time as yer seed me. I'll just diagnose.
Tha goo an' undress thee sel, tak off thee clothes.'

'E prodded me 'ere an' 'e prodded me there,
An' axed me such questions as didn't seem fair.
Says 'e, 'Now me Lad asta gotten thee brass?'
'Fore I know'd were I were I were reet under't gas!

T' Lasses used ter pity me,
An' often ax me out to tea.
But now they won't sit on my knee.
Since I'd my operation. . .

I were a shinin' light, tha knows
From time pubs opened till they closed
It costs a lot now to red me nose.
Since I'd my operation. . .

Then there's the snob, owd Jimmy Cole.
His motter sens me reet up t'pole.
Walk on thee heels an' save thy sole.
Since I'd my operation. . .

An' t' butcher down in Albert Street,
To me he'd give the choicest meat,
But now he gives me Ba-Lambs Feet
Since I'd my operation. . .

Monday's child the tale can tell.
Tuesday's child can rage and yell,
I'm Friday's child, I cough like Hell.
Since I'd my operation. . .

So Rule Britannia
And let me likewise state,
Keep t'money in t' Post Office Bank
And Don't Operate. . . .

WATER RAT

Early in September 1908, Percy Honri was 'made' a member of that exclusive music hall society 'The Grand Order of Water Rats'. The name came from a noted trotter owned by Richard Thornton, founder of the Thornton music hall circuit in the north-east, which had been brought to London and raced on a fifty-fifty basis, winnings and upkeep being shared with a syndicate headed by Joe Elvin and Jack Lotto. In the summer of 1889, after a successful 'coup' over the straight mile down the open Croydon Road, starting at Thornton Heath and finishing at the 'William IV', Streatham, the proceeds defrayed the costs for a Sunday's boating and a dinner at the Magpie Hotel, Sunbury-on-Thames. Here Joe Elvin, Jack Lotto, Wal Pink, Fred and Joe Griffiths, Arthur Forrest, Barney Armstrong, Tom Brantford, George Fairburn and George Harris formed 'Pals of the Water Rat'. Later it was to become the Grand Order of Water Rats, and in April 1890 rules were formulated and a motto adopted – 'Philanthropy and Conviviality'. The officers for the first full year were King Rat: Harry Freeman, Prince Rat: Jack Lotto, Bank Rat: Joe Elvin, Scribe Rat: Wal Pink, and Buck Rat: Fred Harvey. Except for a six-year gap between 1921 and 1927 when activities were suspended due to the upheavals of the war, the Water Rats have remained true to their motto until the present day, and have raised huge sums for charitable causes. They have also had important influences on the politics of the profession, in particular on the creation of the V.A.F. in 1906. The famous ventriloquist Fred Russell wrote a history of the order up to 1947, and in it he pointed out that the pioneer American performers' union, 'White Rats of America', was founded by George Fuller Golden in 1900. George Fuller Golden died in 1912. His book *My Lady Vaudeville*, a fantastic summary of the White Rats movement, describes his British brother Rats as: 'All stars in the merry world of make-believe! All geniuses of laughter and song; all boys – just boys!' It was Grandpa who presented the 'King Rat' chair with its 'Rat' carvings to the order. As Prince Rat in 1930 he composed for one of the Water Rat functions this song:

> Hello all you Pros, I'm just a lad tha' knows
> I left the mill and thought I'd like some fun.
> Cause I'd heard about a job worth five and thirty bob
> From't limelight chap at Hippo Accrington.
> He says give tha knick a wash an' make thysel look posh
> By dressing up in one of Burton's suits.
> Just have a shillin' ad. sai'nt young property lad
> And you'll find yourself up there with them 'golutes'.
> I've worked for Bill O'Farrell,
> I been in front to shout the songs as he should sing.
> Then I work for Daisy Dormer, shall I daddy?
> Up and down I used to sing.
> Then with Coram and young Jerry, I'd a time that was merry
> His figures I'd adore 'em. . . .

You can see Tom Coram's 'Jerry Fisher' figure on display in the London Museum.

THE DRESSING ROOM

Dressing rooms have always been great meeting places for performers and their friends. Whilst visitors are not allowed backstage in a theatre during a performance, and have to leave when the 'half' is called – i.e. 35 minutes before curtain up, in the music halls, these rules are not usually so rigorously enforced, and a twelve-minute turn knew it was always 'on stage' at 7.05 and 9.35 each evening that week – so there was plenty of time to chat!

The old fashioned mother of mine etching by Walter Sickert 1928, of Talbot O'Farrell on stage, *Courtesy Islington Libraries*

Right, en route to panto in the tropics 1936: Avril Angers, Georgie Wood, Mary Honri; below right, Mary Honri 1934; Percy Honri *Era* cartoon 1900

Max Wall has told me of the time he heard Grandpa and George Robey having a private recital in George's dressing room at the Finsbury Park Empire on concertina and violin. Aunt Mary has memories of Harry Tate saying 'Wilkie Bard? He's upstairs – getting older and older!' My aunt also recalls a Percy Honri spoof of quite elaborate proportions dreamt up in a dressing room. It involved Talbot O'Farrell who gained tremendous fame as an Irish tenor, after having little impact as a Scots comic when he made his London debut at the 'Met', Edgware Road, in 1902. Bill O'Farrell continued to earn top billing, and was with Don Ross's *Thanks for the Memory* until a short while before his death in 1952. But Mary remembers:

> One particular time, just after I had started to appear in Grandpa's act, before I played the accordion, but just the piano and sang. . . It was at the Hippodrome, Southend, in August 1926, and the week before Grandpa had had an idea with which he intended to surprise Bill, as he was always called. Grandpa had us both fitted out in exactly the same suits, toppers and sticks, and when at the Monday Bandcall we found that Finlay Dunn with his songs and stories at the piano was also with us, Grandpa took Mrs O'Farrell into the secret and she found an old suit of Bill's and kitted up Finlay.
>
> After Bill's performance at the First House, as usual he went in front of the tabs and made a little speech all about the fact that on Friday night it would be Irish Night and he would be singing a completely different set of songs and – at that moment Finlay stepped through the curtains and announced that he would be playing on an Irish piano and presenting Irish songs – then Grandpa went through and said that he would be playing his Irish concertina – and finally I came through and said that I would be singing an Irish colleen's song. There the four of us stood all dressed alike – black double-breasted coat, shepherd's plaid trousers, white spats and gloves, a grey checked bow tie, a monocle and the grey topper and black stick with a silver knob. We stood there striking the same pose.
>
> Bill was staggered, and before he could say anything the orchestra struck up *The Dear Little Shamrock*, which Father had arranged earlier with the M.D., and we all sang in harmony – and it brought the house down. We did this at every show that week with enormous success, but do you know I don't think that Bill really liked it despite its success – or maybe because of it, for that was the last time that we ever featured on one of Talbot O'Farrell's own variety bills.

My father Baynham has some memories of being backstage at the Palladium. The Palladium has always been the performer's mecca. Since it first opened Grandpa had been playing regular 'return dates' there. On 11 October 1918 he signed a ten-year exclusive contract with the astute and shrewd music hall magnate Charles Gulliver, who became a lifelong personal friend of his. The contract guaranteed Grandpa twenty-six specified weeks' work every year on the L.T.V. circuit, including ten weeks each year at the London Palladium. My father was with him in his dressing room as the 'Khaki Election' results of 1918 came in:

It was the election when Asquith lost his seat at East Fife and I had written some couplets about this sensational result and shown it to Grandpa. He liked it, and told me to get 'Final Editions' of all the evening papers – and write a few more couplets about the election. Then he played over a tune to go with my words. Anyway he put it in at that house, and sang four or five verses. It was a catchy tune too, and by the second verse Horace Sheldon had the whole Palladium orchestra busking it with Percy's concertina.

He only did it the one house, because Charles Gulliver came round to tell him to cut the political couplets out of the act saying: 'A music hall audience is an all-party audience – and your couplets probably offended at least 50 per cent of the patrons!' So that was the only time my lyrics were sung at the Palladium....

Our family link with the Palladium continued when the musical *Our Man Crichton* had an excerpt included in I.T.V.'s *Sunday Night at the London Palladium*. As the 'Reverend John Treherne' with my miniature concertina, I played *Little Darlin'* for Millicent Martin, and my six week old son Paul Simon 'stayed up to watch'. *Our Man Crichton* was set at the turn of the century, and this was a peak period in the story of the halls, with pros dashing from one hall to another.

The craziest club in the world then was the Big Dressing Room at the Tivoli in the Strand. The premier house in George Adney Payne's circuit, all the male stars playing the Gibbons and the Payne circuits would go there first and change into their stage props before starting their evening round. In charge of this room was Fred the Dresser, whose whole aim in life was for the dressing room to always be in perfect order. When he was out of the room, bets would be taken as to the length of time before he saw a farthing-sized piece of paper the comics had put on the floor. It took him usually about fifteen seconds to spot it and put it in the waste bin. The Adelphi is just across the road from where the Tiv used to be, and it was in my dressing room during the run of *Blitz!* that plans for the formation of the Entertainers Rugby Club were first hatched by Paul Haley and myself in April 1963. An enjoyable charity match had been played between Paul's 'Black & White Minstrels XV' and my 'Blitz XV', and since then the Entertainers have raised around £2,000 for charity. I can also claim to have played in the same team as Cliff Morgan, when Cliff guested with the Club!

Up to World War I, a Music Hall Sports Day was regularly held at Herne Hill for the Variety Artistes Benevolent Fund with over £500 offered in prizes – I see that Tom Pacey ran third in the Agents' Race at the 1901 Sports. At the same meeting, Harry Ford won the 120 yards Running Handicap (Artistes only) in 13 seconds. Now the Royal Performance is the principal source of income for the maintenance of Brinsworth – the home for retired performers. This house at Twickenham was bought mainly through the generosity of Joe Elvin, who in 1909 donated £500 towards the cost of the freehold.

The Yorkshireman 1888: far left, Percy Honri as Tommy Tucker; right, Mary Thompson as Margery Daw; far right, Harry Thompson as The Dame

The Dame.

PANTO TIME

The stage manager has given the 'five minute call' to curtain-up. Elsie dashes up the customary nine flights of stone steps to the long narrow dressing room at the top of the theatre that is traditionally allocated to the dancers. A dozen voices seem to be shrieking at once: 'Anyone got a safety pin?' – 'Who's got me pumps?' – 'Hazel, why don't you shut your mouth!' Her friend Connie is standing on a chair with one leg in the sink dabbing on 'wet white'. Seeing Elsie she stops for a moment to shout: 'Coom on, Else – Foreman says blind'll be goin' oop soon and you haven't got your marks on yet.' So runs the story about a couple of mill girls recruited to augment the 'line' in a northern provincial pantomime. It is a story which can be repeated a hundredfold every year and can sometimes provide more amusement than what happens on the stage itself.

In 'Some Pantomime Pedigrees', V. C. Clinton-Baddeley makes the point that when the music hall comedians like Dan Leno and Herbert Campbell were first involved in pantomime, they were '. . . not going to renounce their favourite gags, simply because they find themselves in a new entertainment. Basic humour is inter-national and unkillable. . . .' Whilst they and many others would command higher salaries for their panto seasons, most of the supporting casts were not so lucky. Edith Glynne, a forty year old 'prima donna' sang in Wilson Barrett's Grand Leeds panto The Pretty Princess & the Wicked Old Man of the Sea for an eight-week season in 1886 at a salary of £2 per week. As a 'serio' in 1882, Tom Machin had paid her £7 5s for the week at his Underground Music Hall, Wicker, Sheffield. She also held contracts worth a total of £6 10s for two weeks in September 1886 at the Bradford Old Crown and the Albert Music Halls. On the other hand pantomime has launched many a fledgling 'Beam's Babe' or 'Terry's Juvenile' on a stage career.

Our family associations with pantomime go back at least to 1888, when the Thompson Trio played in Red Riding Hood at the Theatre Royal, Leeds, for Joseph Hobson. Harry played 'Dame Tottie Grey', Mary Thompson was 'Margery Daw' and young Percy was 'Tommy Tucker'. About the same time, W. H. Broad-head's aqua-pantomimes were starting at Blackpool; and later most of the Broadhead halls would show pantomime at Christmas. These were all pantomimes where the 'star-trap' by the left wing regularly catapulted Evil on to a stage enveloped in a magnesium flash and a cacophony of hisses – pantomimes which had the traditional harlequinade, and spectacular transformation scenes. The Yorkshire Post, describing the Leeds panto's 'transformation', said: '. . . It has been evolved from a scene in The Tempest and is illustrative of Ariel, his labours and reward. The idea of the sprite flying on a bat's back singing is very adroitly and pleasingly demonstrated. . . Mr Harry Thompson made a decided hit as Dame Tottie Grey, and one of the best things in the pantomime was his version of "It's English, you know, quite English". . . .'

Some forty-six years later, Mary Honri made her debut as pantomime's youngest 'principal boy', and in 1937 she was in Georgie Wood's pantomime in South Africa, with Avril Angers playing Cinders and Georgie as Buttons. Georgie Wood,

MAX WALL

APPEARING AS "LEOPOLD" IN
"WHITE HORSE INN" ON ICE

"Success" to June.
Max Wall

Above, Max Wall in *White Horse Inn on Ice* 1954
Right, Peter Honri and June Bernice 1957

a master of the sketch on the halls, had been a headliner for twenty years – the archetypal 'little boy' with Dolly Harmer as his 'stage mother'. Writing in *Weekend Review* (8 November 1930), the critic Ivor Brown said: '. . . What a perfect piece of applied art his sketches are, the dialogue being built up to let the boy score gently and without impertinence. . . . Our native compassion is particularly fond of the under-dog which has still a show of spirit and can wag its tail. . . .' He made a perfect Buttons. The *Johannesburg Star* spoke of Georgie's production having 'the authentic atmosphere reaching out over the footlights and enveloping you in the charm of its illusion. . . Mary Honri is in the true tradition of principal boys. Her work is done with an air, she really is the prince of Cinderella's dreams. . . .'

Sixty-four years after the Thompson Trio's Leeds panto, I was playing 'Pop' to my sister Pinkie Honri's 'Goldilocks' in the Denville Players pantomime at South Shields.

My wife June started her career in the massive ice pantomimes at the Empress Hall. Here again one found variety comics like Norman Wisdom, Tommy Trinder and Max Wall crossing over to the lucrative ice shows in the same way as Leno and Campbell had joined the Drury Lane pantomimes. Certainly as extravaganzas the ice pantos have donned the mantle of Drury Lane. But spectacle is not everything, whether in pantomime or musical, and producers would do well to recall Bernard Shaw's comments on the weight given to script compared with splendour:

> . . . If Mr Dan Leno had asked for a 100 guinea tunic to wear during a single walk across the stage, no doubt he would have got it, with a 50 guinea hat and sword-belt to boot. If he had asked for 10 guineas worth of the time of a competent dramatic humorist to provide him with at least one line that might not have been pirated from the nearest Cheap Jack, he would I suspect, have been asked whether he wished to make Drury Lane bankrupt. . . .

What pantomime is complete without its song sheet? The comic has shouted for Charlie to lower the words from the flies. Everyone knows that they will have to do vocal battle with the 'top shelf' or the 'ash-trays'; that the comic will indicate how deaf he is to any efforts we may make, whether we're 'three or ninety three'. Here is Percy Honri's song sheet, that could have been sung by George Jackley at the Lyceum with his shock red wig and his striped trousers, and that extraordinary voice:

> I've a silly ditty I will sing to you.
> Words are awfully pretty never make me blue.
> Took a lot of paper and a lot of ink
> When you've heard me sing it once
> You'll join in – I think.
>
> Pom-Tiddley-Om-Pom – Pom Pom.
> Pom-Tiddley-Om-Pom – Pom Pom.
> Can't complain. That refrain. Gives me pain – once again.

Pom-Tiddley-Om-Pom — Pom Pom.
Pom-Tiddley-Om-Pom — Pom Pom.
Just once more. Let it roar.
Pom-Tiddley-Om-Pom — Pom Pom!

Hardly Shavian perhaps, but then 'a jest's prosperity lies in the ear of him that hears it, never in the tongue of him that makes it'.

Percy Honri's 'Past Prince Rat' medal

9 PLAY OUT MUSIC

THIS is not the last turn of the music hall . . . there are countless thousands more who will in their turn enter and exit smiling. The performer may, in Adam Smith's words, have given a service that 'disappeared in the instant of its performance, leaving behind no tangible, vendible commodity'. But do we really want to judge entertainment by the dry words of an eighteenth-century economist?

Today we have the mechanical means to capture on tape or film a shadowy impression of a particular performance. Posterity no longer needs to rely solely

Cartoon of Peter Honri as the 'Jolly Jester' by Paul Nicholls

Top right, Mr and Mrs W. H. Broadhead, Mr and Mrs Percy Honri, Baynham Honri; right, Mr and Mrs Percy Honri and Mary Honri; below, Harry Thompson and Baynham; below centre, Harry Thompson, Peter and Pinkie Honri; below right, June Bernice and Peter Honri with their children, Sarah, Caroline and Paul

on memory. Variety arts in particular exist through the audience. Their strength is drawn from the public; their skills have grown and developed from the relationship between listener and storyteller – their crafts maintain the continuity of the music hall tradition by this two-way participation.

A book can only try to put a subject into perspective, and in these pages I have attempted this through the eyes of four generations. It has all happened – Harry's harmoniumised tobacco; Percy's meeting with Gaisberg and cutting the first disc; Baynham making the first broadcast from a moving train; Mary and her accordion in France; W. H. Broadhead's 'seventeen envelopes slit open most meticulously'; Nan's buckets full of coppers. It is in that sense a history – not just of my own family, but of the whole family of music hall.

My tasks in writing *Working the Halls* has been made much easier by the patience and help of June and the children. June has ensured that the supply of fibre pens and carbon paper has not outweighed a balanced approach to an exciting task. My children, Sarah, Caroline and Paul, have taken to an author in their midst as casually as they accepted 'Daddy's concertinas and funny voices'. A positive gold-mine of information has come from my father 'Dadda Bay', and from 'Auntie Mary', and I can never thank them enough for their help with thoughts, words, songs and pictures. The fun we have had recording Grandpa's music is our tribute to Percy Honri – 'King of the Concertina'.

No music hall bill is complete without an overture – and what a splendid one has come from the pen of Spike Milligan. Thank you Spike – they don't write tunes like that these days. Every line's a winner! It was extremely kind of Sir Laurence Olivier to allow me to quote his views on microphones and music hall, and of Alan Plater to permit me to use material from his play *The Reluctant Juggler*.

Brian Rust and Bart Langdon have helped discographically; J. O. Blake has done so photographically. Val Elsey, F.R.I.B.A., has drawn a fine impression of a possible recreated 'Old Mahogany Bar' at Wilton's. Helen Grant Ferguson has smilingly coped with the design and has contributed some highly evocative drawings.

A first book is an awesome undertaking and needs encouragement. I have had this in plenty from my publishers, who invited me to write it. I should like to record as well the helpful advice given to me by Peter Cotes, Marius Goring and Don Ross, who are associated with me in our Wilton's Music Hall Trust project.

Music hall has so many facets; it also has so many friends, and my research has underlined for me, too, how many recall our concertina family. Dozens have written or spoken to me, and their contributions have helped in the jigsaw, though adding a list of names does mean that I omit those who helped me 'fill in data' before I thought of authorship! Thank you – Doris Ansell; Len Belmont; Walter Berlin; Harry C. Bond; J. H. Booth; Fred Broadhead; David Cheshire; Gerald Croasdell; John Earl; Captain Harry Grattidge, O.B.E.; Michael Harding; Linda Hornzee; Wilfred Horwood; John Huntley; Hilary Kilner; Eddie Lattimer; Douglas Livingstone; Bill Martin; Jim and Marjorie Mitchell; John Montgomery; Alex Munro; Brian O'Gorman; Patrick Phillips; Peter Plouviez; Marjorie Ristori;

Ted Rogers; Bert Ross; Frances Selby; Mark Shivas; Dr Denis Smith; Max Wall; Neil Wayne; Douglas White; Ken Wilson; Barbara Windebank.

We have a special family whistle, the first two bars of one of Grandpa's jolliest tunes – the one I played and sang coming out of the jack-in-the-box at Richmond Theatre in 1972. The 'Jolly Old Jester' song from Percy Honri's *Concordia* makes ideal 'play out music' – 'Okay Frank – Are the boys all ready? Off we go. . . .'

> I'm a jolly old jester, jester, jester.
> I'm the kind, the sort of man who never brings a frown.
> Bobbin' about like a boat on the rocks
> Just like a jolly old jack in the box.
> I'm the jolly old jester – the jolliest jester in Town!

ARCO 10M

Music for the 'family tune,' *The Jolly Jester*

ACKNOWLEDGEMENTS

The spirit of the music hall lives on in memories, in books, photos and programmes, in posters and scrapbooks, but most of all in the tunes that are part of the British tradition.

As an early member of the British Music Hall Society, now on its Editorial Board, I have obtained much information not only from the Society's own journal *The Call Boy*, but also from back numbers of the other professional papers *The Era*, *The Stage*, *The Encore*, *The Entracte* and *The Performer*.

I acknowledge gratefully the generous assistance given to me by Westminster Central Library, Stafford Central Library, Islington Central Library, William Salt Library, Stafford, and the Alton Library, and by their staffs, and in particular C. A. Elliot, F.L.A., of the Islington Library and H. Dyson, A.L.A., F.R.S.A., of the Stafford Library; also the International Ventriloquist Association, the Grand Order of Water Rats and the British Actors Equity Association (incorporating Variety Artistes Federation).

I have quoted in the text all sources where known including scrapbooks and family letters. The publishers of several music hall autobiographies have been kind enough to permit me to quote from their books. I am grateful in particular to the Bodley Head for the extracts from Arthur Robert's *Fifty Years of Spoff* and to the Hutchinson Publishing Group Limited for the passages from George Mozart's *Limelight* and Charles Coborn's *The Man Who Broke the Bank*.

Music hall historians owe a great debt to hundreds of unnamed reporters who reviewed the performers working the halls.

Most of the illustrations are from my own collection and those of my family, but I am grateful for help in this field from the British Music Hall Society, the Trustees of the National Portrait Gallery, Thames Television, the B.B.C., British Rail, the Greater London Council, Columbia Pictures Ltd, the Leicester Galleries of London, Farnham Repertory Company Ltd, Donmar Productions Ltd and Hutchinson Publishing Group Limited.

Although I have made every effort to account for material used in this book, I apologise for any omissions that may occur. These will be rectified in subsequent editions.

BOOKS OF INTEREST

J. B. Booth, *Old Pink 'Un Days*, Grant Richards, 1924

Charles Coborn, *The Man Who Broke the Bank*, Hutchinson, 1930

Peter Cotes, *George Robey*, Cassell, 1972

Albert Chevalier, *Before I Forget*, T. Fisher Unwin, 1901

V. C. Clinton-Baddeley, *Some Pantomime Pedigrees*, Society of Theatre Research, 1963

Arthur Croxton, *Crowded Nights and Days*, Sampson Low, 1930

Jacques Damase, *Les folies du music hall*, a history of the music hall in Paris from 1914 to the present day, Spring Books, 1970

Peter Davidson (ed), *British Music Hall Songs*

M. Willson Disher, *Winkles and Champagne*, Batsford, 1938

M. Willson Disher (ed), *The Cowells in America*, Oxford, 1934

James Douglas, *Adventures in London*, Cassell, 1909

Era Almanac

Daniel Farson, *Marie Lloyd and Music Hall*, Tom Stacey, 1972

Herman Finck, *My Melodies Memories*, Hutchinson, 1937

John Fisher, *Funny Way to be a Hero*, Muller, 1973

George Gamble, *The 'Halls'*, T. Fisher Unwin, 1901

Peter Gammond, *Your Own, Your Very Own*, Ian Allan, 1971

Douglas Gilbert, *American Vaudeville*, Dover, 1940

Jimmy Glover, *Jimmy Glover – His Book*, Methuen, 1911

George Gray, *Vagaries of a Vagabond*, Heath Cranton, 1930

H. G. Hibbert, *A Playgoer's Memories*, Grant Richards, 1920

H. G. Hibbert, *Fifty Years of a Londoner's Life*, Grant Richards, 1916

Diana Howard, *London Theatres and Music Halls 1850–1950*, Library Association, 1969

Naomi Jacob, *Our Marie*, Hutchinson, 1936

Colin MacInnes, *Sweet Saturday Night*, MacGibbon and Kee, 1967

Raymond Mander and Joe Mitchenson, *British Music Hall: A Story in Pictures*, Studio Vista, 1965

G. J. Mellor, *Poms Poms and Ruffles*, Dalesman, 1966

G. J. Mellor, *Northern Music Hall*, Frank Graham, 1970

W. H. Morton and H. Chance Newton, *Sixty Years Stage Service* (Life of Charles Morton), Gale and Polden, 1905

George Mozart, *Limelight*, Hurst and Blackett, 1938

Ralph Nevill and Charles Edward Jerningham, *Piccadilly to Pall Mall*, Duckworth, 1908

Ronald Pearsall, *Victorian Popular Music*, David and Charles, 1973

George Pearson, *Flashback*, Allen and Unwin, 1957

Harry Randall, *Harry Randall — Old Time Comedian*, Low, n. d.

Arthur Roberts, *Fifty Years of Spoof*, Bodley Head, 1927

George Robey, *Looking Back on Life*, Grant Richards, 1916

Fred Russell, *History of the Grand Order of Water Rats*, G.O.W.R. 1947

Harold Scott, *An English Song Book*, Chapman and Hall, 1925

Harold Scott, *The Early Doors*, Nicholson and Watson, 1946

Emily Soldene, *My Theatrical and Musical Recollections*, Downey 1897

Stage Directory

Stage Year Book

C. Douglas Stuart and A. J. Park, *The Variety Stage*, T. Fisher Unwin, 1895

Bransby Williams, *An Actor's Story*, Chapman and Hall, 1909

J. Hickory Wood, *Dan Leno*, Methuen, 1905

INDEX